I0819200

SOURDOUGH
EVERYTHING

RACHEL PARDOE

SOURDOUGH EVERYTHING

Sweet and Savory Recipes *for* Beautiful Breads and Other Bakes

Publisher Mike Sanders
Art & Design Director William Thomas
Editorial Director Ann Barton
Senior Editor Brook Farling
Editorial Assistant Resham Anand
Designer Joanna Price
Photographer Marianne Rothbauer
Food & Prop Stylist Marianne Rothbauer
Styling Assistant Sarah Farmer
Recipe Tester Thom England
Proofreaders Lisa Himes, Monica Stone
Indexer Johnna VanHoose Dinse

First American Edition, 2026
Published in the United States by DK Publishing
1745 Broadway, 20th Floor, New York, NY 10019

The authorized representative in the EEA is Dorling Kindersley
Verlag GmbH. Arnulfstr. 124, 80636 Munich, Germany

26 27 28 29 30 10 9 8 7 6 5 4 3 2 1
001-348848-MAR2026

A catalog record for this book
is available from the Library of Congress.
ISBN 978-0-5939-6764-5

Printed and bound in China

www.dk.com

This book was made with Forest Stewardship Council™ certified paper – one small step in DK's commitment to a sustainable future.
Learn more at
www.dk.com/uk/information/sustainability

To my children, whose presence is a daily lesson in joy, curiosity, and the magic of the little things.

Contents

9 Introduction

CHAPTER 1
Getting Started • 11

12 Using this Book
15 All about Sourdough Starter
16 Making Your Own Sourdough Starter
18 Types of Sourdough Starter
20 Sourdough Enzo Feeding Regimen
25 Baker's Percentages
26 Frequently Asked Questions about Sourdough Starter
29 Tools

CHAPTER 2
Gluten Development, Proofing, and Shaping • 31

32 Techniques for Developing Gluten
38 Understanding Proofing
42 Frequently Asked Questions about Proofing
46 Shaping Sourdough

CHAPTER 3
Basic Sourdough Loaves • 51

52 Sourdough Enzo Master Loaf
55 Sourdough Enzo Whole Wheat Loaf
56 Rye-Blend Loaf
59 Rugbrød

CHAPTER 4
Inclusions • 61

62 Lemon Poppyseed Loaf
65 Browned Butter and Flaxseed Loaf
66 Maple Oat Porridge Loaf
69 Candied Ginger and Thyme Loaf
70 Orange Cranberry Loaf
73 Jalapeño Cheddar Loaf
74 Cinnamon-Raisin Swirl Loaf

CHAPTER 5
Enriched Loaves • 77

78 Soft White Sandwich Bread
81 Honey Whole Wheat Sandwich Bread
82 Fluffy Challah Bread
84 Buttery Brioche
87 Enriched Cinnamon-Raisin Swirl Loaf

CHAPTER 6
Rolls and Buns • 89

90 Demi-Baguettes
93 Soft Dinner Rolls
94 Soft Burger Buns
97 Garlic Knots
98 Ciabatta
101 Pan de Cristal
102 English Muffins
105 Montreal-Style Bagels
106 Salt Butter Rolls (Shio Pan)
109 Pain Viennois
110 German Soft Pretzels
113 Turkish Simits

CHAPTER 7
Flatbreads • 115

116 Tomato-Rosemary Focaccia
119 Apple-Cinnamon Focaccia
120 Peach and Goat Cheese Focaccia
123 Pala Romana

124 Same-Day Sourdough Naan
127 Pocket Pitas
128 Fluffy Turkish Pides
130 Neapolitan-Style Sourdough Pizzas
132 Garlic Fingers with Donair Sauce
135 Soft Tortillas
136 Moroccan-Style Msemen
139 Buttery Paratha

CHAPTER 8
Sweet Sourdough Breads • 141

142 Fluffy Chocolate Babka
144 Fluffy Poppyseed Babka
146 Fluffy Cinnamon Babka
148 Apple Butter and Candied Walnut Wool Roll
151 Nutella-Filled Buns
152 Plum-Filled Donuts (Polish Pączki)
154 Fluffy Overnight Cinnamon Buns
156 Cardamom Knots
158 Buttery Croissants
161 Pain aux Raisins
165 Pumpkin Chocolate Buns
166 Lemon Cardamom Buns

CHAPTER 9
Sourdough-Discard Breads • 169

170 Morning Crumpets
173 Two-Shores Oatcakes
174 My Favorite Banana Bread
177 Fluffy Pancakes
178 Golden Waffles
181 Classic Buttermilk Scones
182 Raisin Bran Muffins
185 Fudgy Brownies
186 Double Chocolate Brownie Cookies
189 Cloud Crullers
190 Chewy Chocolate Chip Cookies
193 Chewy Peanut Butter Cookies
194 Linzer Cookies
196 Flaky Strawberry Turnovers
198 Flaky Apple Turnovers
201 Lemon Poke Loaf
202 Phyllo Ricotta Triangles
205 Seedy Crackers
206 Potato Gnocchi
209 Enzo's Pasta
210 Cornbread Muffins

CHAPTER 10
Decorating Sourdough Bread • 213

215 Bread Decorating Tools
216 Scoring
220 Creating Seed Designs
222 Decorating with Stencils, Doilies, and Textured Cloths
226 Creating Three-Dimensional Paint Designs
229 Braiding

231 Acknowledgments
232 Index
240 About the Author

Dear Reader,

Welcome to *Sourdough Everything*.

I'm so grateful you've picked up this book. Whether you're brand new to sourdough, familiar with the basics, or a sourdough aficionado, I hope this book meets you exactly where you are and gives you the knowledge and confidence to keep going.

When I was first gifted a little jar of starter by my neighbor, I had no idea how deeply it would root itself into my life. I spent weeks soaking up any information I could about sourdough: reading blog posts and watching YouTube tutorials, in a near state of paralysis about making a loaf. Taking that first step felt like such a *big deal* for the simple fear of failure. (The reality was, the failures were where a lot of my knowledge was gained.) When I finally baked my first loaf, I clung to the same ritualistic process, week after week, determined to get it right. For nearly a year, I refused to bake anything else. That period—my personal artisan-loaf purgatory, as I like to think of it—became more than just trial and error, it became my creative outlet. I poured myself into every loaf, decorating to my heart's content. It was through that process that *Sourdough Enzo* (the handle for my social media accounts and named after my starter) came to life.

This book is designed to make sourdough accessible, easy to understand, and versatile—because it's not just about open crumbs, oven spring, and blistered crusts (although those are great, too), it's also about discovering the joy of making your own sourdough, not worrying about perfection, and embracing the process of learning from the mistakes while enjoying every step along the way.

Inside you'll find clear instructions, explanations, and my best tips to help you succeed in your sourdough journey. The first chapter walks you through starter care, including what to expect and how to troubleshoot when things get confusing. The second dives into proofing—one of the most important aspects of sourdough success. (I spent far too long underproofing my loaves, and I hope that, armed with the knowledge from this book, you can avoid a similar fate!) From there, you'll find a collection of my favorite recipes—everything from classic loaves and enriched doughs to sourdough-discard recipes. There's an entire chapter on scoring and embellishing bread, where I share the artistic side of sourdough that kept me grounded when everything else in life felt chaotic. Because that's what this journey has been for me—a place of peace ... a quiet ritual ... a small but steady source of creation and joy in uncertain times. I hope it brings you that same kind of comfort.

So don't be afraid to start. Don't wait for perfect conditions or the "right" time. Just begin. Trust your instincts, and know that every loaf—no matter how it turns out—is part of the process.

Warmly,

CHAPTER 1

Getting Started

Using This Book

This book is meant to be a friendly, flexible guide to help you achieve sourdough success, from your very first loaf to more advanced bakes. While this is a sourdough bread–baking book and not every recipe will use sourdough starter as a form of leavening, you can expect that all of the recipes contained in this book will use some form of sourdough in the process.

I have extensive experience in baking sourdough simply due to the frequency and years I have been baking. That said, I am *not* a professional pastry chef or trained baker. I am a home baker, and these recipes were developed in my own kitchen to share with family and friends. They are not mass produced or bakery tested, just lovingly home-tested.

This book is meant to be a guide. There is always room to adjust, adapt, and experiment when it comes to sourdough baking—in fact, I *encourage* experimentation, as that is part of the journey and the joy. It is important to know, however, that any changes to these recipes may affect the dough's flavor or texture.

Some of the doughs in this book are higher hydration and may require a bit of confidence with dough handling. If a dough feels too wet or sticky, feel free to sprinkle it with additional flour to make things more manageable. My goal is to help build your confidence, not intimidate.

Most recipes call for active (at peak) 100%-hydration active sourdough starter. That means you'll need to plan ahead to ensure your starter is active and ready to be used for the recipe. This usually means that you should feed your starter several hours prior to starting the recipe to ensure that it is ripe and ready to go when you are ready to make the dough. In the cases where I make a levain, I will provide the specific instructions required in that particular recipe.

Remember, experimentation is part of the journey and part of the joy. You'll learn as you go. But more than anything, don't stress. Enjoy the process. Savor the peace that comes with working dough in your hands and creating something beautiful from scratch.

All about Sourdough Starter

Sourdough starter is the core of any sourdough bread recipe. Below you will learn what it is, what it's comprised of, and how it gives rise to your breads. Whether you're new to sourdough or want to have a better grasp of your starter, the following guide walks you through the basics and the science behind it.

What is Sourdough Starter?

Sourdough starter is a natural leavening agent created by mixing just flour and water. This combination is allowed to sit for a period of time in order to absorb the ambient (wild) yeast and bacteria that is in the air around us, which in turn gives rise to your dough. Sourdough starter has been used to leaven breads for thousands of years. In fact, one of the oldest sourdough breads, excavated in Switzerland, dates back to 3700 BC!

Because it contains ambient yeast and bacteria, sourdough starter is a *living* organism, which means it requires regular feeding to ensure it stays alive and is able to leaven your breads. If you do not feed it, it will die. While the process of making sourdough starter is relatively simple, it can take time and patience.

Understanding Sourdough Starter (The Science of Starter)

Most sourdough starters are comprised of a mixture of flour, water, and microorganisms (yeasts, lactic acid bacteria, and acetic acid bacteria). These microorganisms that are a part of your starter come from the air, your starter jar, and even the mixing utensil you use. The microorganisms feed off the flour and water, allowing them to propagate and grow.

Yeast primarily helps to leaven your dough. As the yeast feeds, it proliferates and converts the simple carbohydrates from the flour into carbon dioxide and ethanol (alcohol). The carbon dioxide is what creates the bubbles in your starter and dough. Yeast thrives in warmer environments, and as yeast is the primary leavening agent in sourdough, dough that is proofed in a warm environment will rise quickly.

Lactic acid bacteria and acetic acid bacteria are smaller and about 100 times more prolific in a sourdough starter. Like the yeast in your sourdough culture, the bacteria also consume the simple carbohydrates and produce lactic acid and acetic acid (although some also produce ethanol), which adds the conventional "sour" flavor to your sourdough. Lactic acid tends to produce a milder, yogurt-like sour profile, and acetic acid produces a sharper, vinegar-like sour profile. The presence of the bacteria has several benefits, including extending the shelf life of your bread, but also making the sourdough easier to digest, which helps support a healthy gut microbiome.

What is the Best Way to Store Sourdough Bread?

Many people suggest storing regular sourdough in a linen bag or beeswax-lined bag. My preference is to store it in a resealable plastic bag. I find this prevents the loaf from going stale faster. Using a paper, linen, or beeswax-lined bag means that air is more likely to permeate the bag. Exposure to air will make the bread go stale faster!

I do not recommend refrigerating bread. While refrigerated bread is less likely to grow mold, refrigeration speeds up the recrystallization (the regrouping of starches into a crystalline structure), causing it to harden and making the bread go stale faster. If you wish to preserve the bread, simply slice and freeze it. Storing the bread in a resealable bag in the freezer for up to 2 months will ensure optimum freshness.

None of the recipes in this book contain any preservatives. Therefore, you will notice that the breads do not retain their softness over time, even when they're stored in a resealable bag at room temperature. Because of this, I prefer to warm my bread in the microwave or in the toaster, depending on the preferred end result.

Making Your Own Sourdough Starter

In order to make the recipes in this book, you will need a healthy sourdough starter. While you can certainly obtain a starter from a friend or neighborhood bakery, or purchase a dehydrated starter online and reactivate it at home, I will walk you through the process of making your own.

What you will need:

Ingredients
Rye flour
All-purpose flour
Warm tap water, no warmer than 100°F (38°C) (see Notes)

Equipment
Digital kitchen scale
Stainless-steel spoon or knife
Two straight-sided clear glass jars (500ml each)
Plastic wrap or bamboo lid fitted to the glass jars

Day 1:
Place one of the jars on your digital scale and tare it (zero it by pressing the tare button). To the jar, add 25 grams of the rye flour and 25 grams of the warm tap water. Mix with a stainless-steel spoon or knife until they are fully incorporated. Cover the jar with the bamboo lid or plastic wrap and let it rest for 24 hours at a warm room temperature (anything above 70°F [21°C]).

Days 2 and 3:
If after 24 hours, you do not see any fermentation activity (bubbles appearing at the sides and top of the jar), wait another 12 to 24 hours until you start to see fermentation. Once you start to see bubbles, you will start the discard process. Transfer 25 grams of the mixture to the clean glass jar. (You can discard the remainder or keep it to make one of the sourdough-discard recipes in this book.) To the 25-gram mixture, add 15 grams all-purpose flour, 10 grams rye flour, and 25 grams warm tap water. Mix until fully incorporated. Cover the jar with the bamboo lid or plastic wrap and let it rest for 24 hours at a warm room temperature. Clean the first glass jar to prepare for the next day.

Days 3 or 4:
After 24 hours, you may notice similar or more activity in the form of more bubbles visible on the sides and top of the glass jar. You may even notice a rise in the mixture. At this point, transfer 25 grams of the mixture to the clean glass jar and discard the remainder. To the 25-gram mixture, add 20 grams all-purpose flour, 5 grams rye flour, and 25 grams warm tap water. Mix until fully incorporated. Cover the jar with the bamboo lid or with plastic wrap and let it rest for 24 hours at a warm room temperature. Clean the glass jar from which you discarded the remainder.

Day 4 or 5:
If you see more bubbles and more rise, transfer 25 grams of the mixture to the clean glass jar and discard the remainder. To the 25-gram mixture, add 25 grams all-purpose flour and 25 grams warm tap water. Mix until fully incorporated. Cover with the bamboo lid or with plastic wrap and let it rest for 24 hours at a warm room temperature. Clean the glass jar from which you discarded the remainder.

Day 5 or 6:
Transfer 25 grams of the mixture to the clean glass jar and discard the remainder. To the 25-gram mixture, add 25 grams all-purpose flour and 25 grams warm tap water. Mix until fully incorporated. Cover with the bamboo lid or with plastic wrap and let it rest for 12 hours at warm room temperature.

Days 6 and 7 (and onward):
Keeping the full 50 grams in the jar, add 50 grams all-purpose flour and 50 grams warm tap water. Mix until fully incorporated. Cover with a bamboo lid or with plastic wrap and let it rest for 12 hours at a warm room temperature. (For an ongoing feeding schedule, see my feeding regime on page 20.)

How Do I Know When My Starter Is Ready to Bake With?

After this prolonged process of creating your own starter, you will want to ensure that it is ready to use for baking. Without a healthy, active starter, you will not be able to produce a beautiful loaf of sourdough!

A healthy, active starter should ...

- double (or more) in size when at peak.
- have apparent bubbles on the sides and top of the jar.
- have a tangy (but not overly sour) aroma.

A starter that is not ready to bake with may ...

- have little to no rise.
- remain dense, with no visible air bubbles.
- have an overly sour aroma or smell just of flour.

Types of Sourdough Starter

There are several types of sourdough starters, each offering unique benefits depending on how they're maintained and what they're used for. In this section, I focus on naturally leavened starters rather than preferments like *poolish* or *biga*, which rely on commercial yeast and are outside the scope of this book.

My go-to is a regular all-purpose starter for its versatility, ease of use, and ability to be built into a levain. Occasionally, I'll prepare a stiff starter when working with enriched doughs that require a stronger crumb structure. The chart that follows outlines some of the most common types of sourdough starters, highlighting their typical hydration levels, flour types, texture, common uses, and what types of bread they are best suited for.

While there's no single "best" type of sourdough starter, my own personal preference is to maintain a regular starter and build from that a levain, if needed. I like to keep things simple, and for me, that means working with a single dependable (regular, all-purpose) starter that can adapt to whatever I'm baking. Once you understand how each type functions, you'll find it easier to choose the right one. Or you can confidently stick with just one and let technique do the heavy lifting!

Notes:

- It's easier to make a sourdough starter when it is in a warm environment. In temperatures below 66°F (19°C), your starter will grow much slower and will show less activity. This process requires more patience and time.
- Using warm filtered water may also help to speed up the growth of your sourdough culture. Since tap water contains chlorine, it may weaken the yeast in your culture.

	Regular Starter	*Liquid Starter*	*Stiff Starter*	*Pasta Madre*
Hydration	100%	200–400%	50–60%	30–50%
Flour	All-purpose, Bread, Rye, Whole wheat, Rice, Potato flake	Bread, Rye, Whole wheat	All-purpose, Bread, Rye, Whole wheat	All-purpose, Bread
Texture	Batter-like	Separated: water sits on top of flour mixture	Similar to bread dough	Stiff, kneadable
Types of bread	Most artisan sourdough breads, baguettes, sandwich loaves, enriched breads, laminated doughs	Most artisan sourdough breads, baguettes	Most enriched breads, laminated doughs	Most known for use in panettone, can be used in enriched doughs
Uses	Depending on quantity used, can offer a mild to a very tangy flavor profile	Can offer a more yogurt-y flavor profile	Can offer a milder flavor profile and stronger structure to the crumb	Very mild flavor profile

Sourdough Enzo Feeding Regimen

Because sourdough starter is a living culture, it needs to be cared for and fed regularly to maintain its strength and leavening power. While there are workarounds if you're away for an extended period of time (see FAQs on page 26), keeping a consistent feeding schedule will help your starter stay healthy and reliable.

If you're baking daily or several times a week (as many commercial bakeries or cottage bakers do), keeping your starter at room temperature at all times and maintaining a daily or twice-daily feeding regime is ideal. However, if you are like me and baking sourdough once or maybe twice a week, storing your starter in the refrigerator between uses is an easier, less time-consuming, and less wasteful process. Here are some tips for keeping your starter healthy and thriving.

Feeding and Storing Your Starter

Once a week, before I go to bed, I pull my starter from the refrigerator and feed it according to my needs. My typical feeding ratio is 1:4:4 (1 part starter, 4 parts water, 4 parts flour). If it is particularly warm in the house, I may adjust this ratio to 1:5:5. This feeding maintains a 100%-hydration starter, meaning the quantities of flour and the water are the same. (To find out more about baker's percentages, see page 25.) Feeding with a higher ratio ensures that the starter will be at its peak and ready for use in the morning the following day, as opposed to the middle of the night. A lower ratio like 1:1:1 will produce a starter that peaks much quicker, sometimes in just a few hours.

In the morning, I use as much starter as I need for my dough and place the remaining starter—while it's still peaked—back in the refrigerator. I can use this starter for leavening bread over the next 3 to 6 days without refeeding or bringing it up to room temperature.

My General Feeding Schedule

Here is the general schedule that I use, which may vary slightly depending on how warm it is in my house.

The evening before mixing the dough (between 8 p.m. and 10 p.m.):

1. Pull the starter from the refrigerator and pour off any hooch (the liquid that forms on top of your starter, which might look muddy, gray, or brown) into the sink.
2. Place the amount of starter that I require into a medium bowl and use a digital scale to weigh it. (See *Feeding Quantity Guide*.)
3. Into the same bowl, measure out the water and flour. (See *Feeding Quantity Guide*.)
4. Stir until completely combined and no lumps remain.
5. Return the mixed starter to the vessel that you usually use or an appropriately sized vessel for the amount of starter you have. You want to allow enough space for it to rise 2 to 3 times in volume.
6. Cover the vessel loosely with a lid. (I have a glass jar with a bamboo lid that has a rubber stopper.) Set it aside at room temperature to rise overnight. (It can be helpful to place a rubber band at the level of the starter so that you can track growth.)

The next morning (between 7 a.m. and 9 a.m.):

Check to see if the starter has peaked.

- **Not yet peaked:** A starter that has not yet reached peak will have a domed appearance, indicating that it is still growing. You may also notice large bubbles on the surface and small-to-medium ones on the sides if you are using a transparent vessel. If the starter has a domed appearance, allow it to remain at room temperature until it has peaked. Continue checking on it periodically.
- **At peak:** A starter that has peaked will have a flat top and large visible bubbles near the surface and on the sides. At this point it is ready to be used for mixing dough. If you are not ready to use it at this point, pop the covered vessel in the fridge until you are ready to use it.
- **Past peak:** A starter that is past its peak and has started to fall will show streaks on the vessel from where it once rose and has started to fall. It also might appear slightly concave. (It is still okay to use if it has fallen.) You may use it for mixing dough at this point. If you are not ready to use it yet, pop the covered vessel in the refrigerator until you are ready to use it.

  Note that a starter that has been placed in the refrigerator after it has started to fall will require refeeding sooner than a starter that is placed in the refrigerator at its peak.

Feeding Quantity Guide (1:4:4 ratio)
Includes amount to save for future feedings (15 to 30 grams)

Final Starter Needed for Baking	*Starter (1 part)*	*Water (4 parts)*	*Flour (4 parts)*	*Total Weight*	*Remainder*
100g	15g	60g	60g	135g	35g
150g	20g	80g	80g	180g	30g
200g	25g	100g	100g	225g	25g
250g	30g	120g	120g	270g	20g
300g	35g	140g	140g	315g	15g

Using Your Starter from the Refrigerator

Keeping your starter in the refrigerator inherently changes the texture as compared to when you're using it as soon as it peaks at room temperature. If you're using it as soon as it peaks after feeding, it will break easily and may also appear runny.

How to know if your starter can be used immediately after pulling it from the refrigerator:

- The starter has large visible bubbles throughout.
- The starter is still very glutinous and can stretch without immediately breaking.
- The starter is very viscous, sticky, thick, and not runny.
- The starter has a pleasant, tangy odor and doesn't smell too sour.
- The starter has not developed any hooch (or brown liquid) on the surface.

How to know if your starter requires refeeding after pulling it from the refrigerator:

- There are only small bubbles or no visible bubbles on the surface.
- The starter breaks easily, showing minimal glutinous structure.
- The starter is runny and not very viscous, sticky, or thick.
- The starter has a strong sour odor similar to nail polish remover or acetone.
- Hooch is present on the surface of the starter.

	Use your starter	*Feed your starter*
Bubbles	Large visible bubbles	Small or no visible bubbles
Gluten	Very glutinous and can stretch without immediately breaking	Breaks easily, minimal gluten structure
Texture	Viscous, sticky, and thick Not runny	Not very viscous or thick Runny
Odor	Pleasant, tangy odor Doesn't smell too sour	May smell like acetone Strong sour odor
Hooch	No presence of hooch	May have hooch

Baker's Percentages

Baker's percentages (sometimes called *baker's math*) is a system in which every ingredient in a recipe is expressed as a percentage of the total flour weight. To calculate a percentage, divide the ingredient weight by the flour weight, then multiply by 100.

When bakers talk about "hydration" in the context of sourdough, they're referring to baker's percentages. You may have heard phrases like "high-hydration dough" or "80%-hydration loaf," but these are all shorthand for how much water (or liquid) is used in relation to the total flour in the dough. Here are some examples hydration percentages:

Total Liquid	*Total Flour*	*Hydration %*
300g	500g	60%
350g	500g	70%
400g	500g	80%

Baker's percentages aren't just used to calculate hydration—they apply to all ingredients in the dough. For example, a typical artisan loaf of sourdough bread contains about 2 percent salt. Inclusion percentages, such as nuts or dried fruit, usually range from 15 to 20 percent. (I'm personally a fan of loading doughs up with add-ins, so take that inclusions percentage range with a grain of salt—pun intended.) Here are some examples of salt percentages:

Total Salt	*Total Flour*	*Salt %*
10g	500g	2%
12g	600g	2%
20g	1000	2%

Frequently Asked Questions About Sourdough Starter

If you have ever second-guessed your starter or found yourself wondering if something is normal, you're not alone. In this section, I've answered the most common questions I hear as a sourdough baker to help you feel more confident in caring for your starter.

What type of flour should I use to start my starter?

It is generally recommended to start a sourdough starter with a whole-grain flour like rye or whole wheat. The reason for this is that these flours are more nutrient dense, which helps accelerate fermentative activity. Once your starter demonstrates consistent activity, you can transition to an all-purpose flour if you so choose.

What type of flour should I use to feed my starter?

That depends on your personal preference. Many people have multiple starters (rye, whole wheat, all-purpose—which they feed with that specific type of flour) depending on what they are using them for. For simplicity, I keep one starter and feed it all-purpose flour.

Can I use tap water to feed my starter?

Yes! I exclusively feed my starter with (potable) tap water.

What is the liquid that forms on top of my starter, and should I discard it?

The liquid that forms on top of your starter, which might look muddy, gray, or brown, is called *hooch*. It is a byproduct of fermentation and is made up of alcohol and water. When your starter has consumed all the food available, it causes a buildup of alcohol, which results in the formation of hooch. You can stir the hooch back into the starter when you feed it or you can pour it off. If you find that it smells quite strong or there is quite a lot of it, I would recommend pouring it off.

What is the "float test"?

The float test is a method of determining whether your starter is ready to be used to make dough. To perform the float test, fill a glass or bowl with room-temperature water. Scoop a teaspoonful of (unstirred) starter from the top of the container and gently drop it into the water. If it floats, your starter should be ready to leaven dough; if it sinks, it either hasn't peaked, has peaked and deflated, or was stirred prior to putting it into the glass. (Note that if you have an all-rye starter, the float test may not be effective at determining whether it is ready to use as they are heavier and may sink even when peaked.)

How do I know when my starter is ready to use?

The float test alone will not determine if your starter is ready to use. It's important to remember the other cues that help to determine whether your starter is ready to use. A healthy, active starter should:

- Double (or more) in size when at its peak.
- Have apparent bubbles on the sides and top of the jar.
- Have a tangy but not overly sour aroma.

Do I need to discard some starter every time I feed it?

This depends on how you maintain your starter. If you maintain a lot of starter and do not use nearly all of it, you may have to discard some in order to feed it a proper ratio. If you just have a small remainder of starter, you may not need to discard at all.

Can I store my starter in the refrigerator?

Absolutely! See page 20, which describes my feeding regimen.

Can I use my starter straight from the refrigerator?

Absolutely! I often use my starter straight from the refrigerator to leaven dough. It is necessary to know whether the starter is still active. See page 22 for details on how to determine if the starter is active.

What do I do if my starter develops mold?

Unfortunately, if your starter develops mold (pink, orange, or fuzzy growth), it has to be discarded since mold can be harmful.

Can I revive a neglected starter?

Usually, yes. Begin by discarding until just 20 grams remain, then feed the remaining starter a 1:1:1 ratio once daily for 3 days and then twice daily until it becomes active again.

What is the difference between a levain and starter?

A levain is a single-use offshoot of your sourdough starter. To create one, you'll remove a portion of your starter, feed it according to the recipe directions, then use all of it for your bake. This means you're feeding both your starter and its offshoot, which can feel redundant and create more dishes. While building a levain is common in many recipes, my personal preference is to do a bulk feed of my starter and once it reaches its peak, pull directly from that to make my doughs. This streamlines the process, removes the extra step of building a separate levain, and reduces the number of dishes used.

My starter smells funny. Is that okay?

Every starter will inherently smell a little bit different as it is composed of the ambient yeast and bacteria in your home environment. It also may smell slightly differently depending on the flour that you feed it. In fact, I fed my starter with an all-purpose flour from a local mill and found that it produced a sulfurous odor. When I switched to a different all-purpose flour, the odor went away! Most starters have a pleasant, tangy odor that is slightly sour. If your starter smells extremely sour or like acetone, it needs to be fed!

How do I make more starter if I need more for a recipe than I currently have on hand?

Creating more starter is a simple matter of feeding your starter more flour and water. If you typically feed your starter a ratio of 1:1:1 (starter: flour: water), you may need to bump up that ratio to 1:5:5, depending on how much starter you begin with, in order to create additional starter.

When does the starter become discard?

Once you notice small or few bubbles, easy breakage, a runny texture, a sour and acetone-like odor, and hooch, the starter has reached a state where it will be far less effective at leavening dough. When the starter has reached this point, it may be considered "discard." While it may still have some leavening power, you may notice it takes a lot longer to proof the dough and the resulting loaf will be considerably more sour. At this point, it's best to either feed it back to strength or repurpose it in discard recipes.

Baking Tools

The beauty of sourdough is its simplicity. All you really need are the basic ingredients: flour, water, and salt (and sometimes eggs, butter, and sugar for enrichment); and the basic tools: a bowl and an oven. However, there are a few tools that can greatly simplify the process.

Banneton

A banneton helps the dough stay in a specific shape while it finishes proofing. A simple bowl can do the trick; however, a banneton will help prevent moisture from developing on the dough, which can result in a wet dough that is more difficult to score. I have tried cane, wicker, and rope bannetons, and they all work well for proofing sourdough. A round banneton will make a boule, and an oval banneton will make a batard.

Bench scraper

A solid, stainless-steel bench scraper makes shaping bread much easier. When making high-hydration loaves, using a bench scraper to help shape the dough is often easier (and less sticky) than using your hands. It also helps you cut and divide the dough into portions.

Bowl covers with polyurethane backs

A bowl cover is an easy and reusable tool you can use to proof your dough. Bowl covers with polyurethane backs help ensure the dough will not form a skin due to the surface being exposed to air. (I love my Wild Clementine bowl covers.)

Bread lame

A bread lame makes sourdough scoring much easier. You'll want to score (cut) dough prior to baking to help the loaf expand. The dough will expand at its weakest point when you bake it, and cutting the dough with a bread lame (or a very sharp knife) will create that point of expansion. There are several types of bread lames available, but I prefer one that allows me to get as close to the dough as possible when performing decorative scores. (I use a Wire Monkey UFO lame with a sharp razor blade for scoring.)

Digital scale

If there is one tool I recommend for any baker, it's a digital scale. Digital scales offer the precision necessary for making sourdough bread and feeding your starter. While cup measures may seem simpler, a cup of flour can vary in weight from 120 grams (spooned and leveled) to 200 grams (packed). It's for this reason that the precision of a digital scale is also esssential when feeding your sourdough starter. If you're making a 100%-hydration starter, you will need to have a feeding ratio of 1:1 by weight, and a scale offers this level of precision since one cup of flour is not equal to one cup of water. You will find that most sourdough recipes use grams when measuring ingredients.

Digital thermometer

A digital thermometer allows accurate measurement of the internal temperature of loaves to ensure they are fully baked. While you can knock on the bottom of a regular sourdough loaf to see if it is fully baked (if it sounds hollow, it is baked), enriched loaves require the precision of a thermometer to ensure you do not underbake the loaves.

Dutch oven or equivalent cast-iron bread cloche

While using a cast-iron bread cloche is not essential, it does ensure the containment of steam that results in a good rise (or oven spring) on a basic, non-enriched sourdough loaf. When baking sourdough, steam allows the loaf to fully expand. If steam is not introduced at the beginning stage of baking, a hard crust will form on the loaf, preventing the loaf from reaching its full expansion potential. Some people bypass the use of a cast-iron cloche by "open baking" in the oven and keeping a tray of water at the bottom of the oven. I have had varying degrees of success using this method simply because my oven cannot contain the steam. I always found best success when using my Fourneau Grande bread oven. The Fourneau Grande allows me to do my 7-minute score (p. 219) without having to lift a heavy Dutch oven in and out of the oven.

Loaf pan

If you're making a sandwich loaf, a formed brioche, or even a formed sourdough loaf, a loaf pan will be necessary. I have a Pullman loaf pan with a lid, as well as several open-top loaf pans. My preferred size of Pullman loaf pan is 8.5 × 4.75 × 4.375-inches (22 × 12 × 11cm), and it's the size that I use in several recipes in this book.

Silicone or plastic bowl scraper

A flexible silicone or plastic bowl scraper helps you cleanly gather dough from the sides of a bowl and incorporate any bits that would otherwise be left behind. It keeps your dough mass together, minimizes waste, and makes cleanup so much easier.

CHAPTER 2

Gluten Development, Proofing, and Shaping

Techniques for Developing Gluten

A key component in successful bread making is developing gluten. While not every bread requires a strong gluten network, it is essential for achieving fluffy, shreddable enriched loaves or a soft, open-crumb sourdough bread.

There are a variety of ways to achieve a strong dough with well-developed gluten, and the method you choose will depend on the type of dough you are working with. Here are some of the different methods for developing gluten.

Kneading (By Hand)

The most traditional way to develop gluten is through hand-kneading—physically pushing and folding the dough repeatedly. Kneading by hand is a slower process than mechanical kneading and can be physically demanding. While kneading by hand works well for most doughs, with higher-hydration doughs, the stickiness can make kneading cumbersome. Kneading by hand is recommended for dough hydrations of less than 65 percent.

Kneading (Mechanical)

There are a variety of mechanical mixers that can aid in the development of gluten. I use a KitchenAid stand mixer with a dough hook attachment to mix my doughs—it saves time, reduces strain on your hands and wrists, and allows you to multitask while the machine does the work. A stand mixer is an easy and efficient replacement for kneading by hand. Mechanical kneading is suitable for most doughs, including high hydration and enriched doughs. Just be careful not to overmix, especially with enriched doughs, which can break down if overworked.

Time

The passage of time itself helps to develop gluten. Some recipes require an *autolyse* step where the flour and water are mixed and allowed to rest for anywhere from 30 minutes to several hours prior to adding the starter and the salt. Resting the dough allows the gluten matrix to form, which aids in the development of dough strength later on. I autolyse my dough during the summer months when I know the warmer ambient environment will cause my dough to proof a lot faster after I add my starter. Autolysis is also effective for higher hydration doughs, as it gives more time for the flour to properly absorb the water.

Stretch-and-Fold

A stretch-and-fold is a clean, simple, and brief method in which to develop gluten and is best used on high-hydration doughs. It is usually done several times over the course of 2 to 3 hours during bulk fermentation. Stretch-and-folds are done after the dough has been mixed and then rested for 30 to 60 minutes.

1. To perform a stretch-and-fold, moisten your hands lightly with water to prevent sticking. Reach under one edge of the dough in the bowl and gently lift it up until you feel some resistance (see image 1). (Do not continue pulling if the dough tears.)
2. Fold the stretched edge to the opposite side of the bowl (see image 2).
3. Turn the bowl a quarter turn and repeat the stretching and folding process on all four sides of the bowl. Cover the bowl and proceed as per the recipe (see image 3).

1

2

3

Coil Fold

A coil fold is similar to a stretch-and-fold, but it offers a gentler way in which to develop gluten. This method minimizes tearing and incorporates more tension compared to a stretch-and-fold. It is also best used on high-hydration doughs, and is done several times over the course of 2 to 3 hours. I use a combination of both stretch-and-folds and coil folds throughout this book. Coil folds are completed after the dough has been mixed and then rested for 30 to 60 minutes.

With each progressive coil fold and rest, you will notice that the dough becomes more taut, more cohesive, and easier to handle. Higher-hydration doughs may benefit from more coil folds.

1. To perform a coil fold, moisten your hands lightly with water to prevent sticking. Gently slide both hands into the bowl and under the middle of the dough (see image 1).
2. Lift the dough straight up from the center, letting the top and bottom sections of the dough naturally stretch downward with their own weight (see image 2). (If you visually divide the bowl into quadrants, imagine a top and bottom quadrant and two side quadrants.)
3. Fold the dough toward the top quadrant. Reach under the middle of the dough again, lifting the dough straight up from the center, and then fold the dough toward the bottom quadrant (see image 3).
4. Rotate the bowl a quarter turn and repeat the process. Cover the bowl and proceed as per the recipe.

Slap-and-Fold

While my preference is to use stretch-and-fold or coil fold to avoid dirtying a countertop, a slap-and-fold is especially effective for helping very high-hydration doughs and enriched doughs vigorously develop gluten. (Your dough should already be mixed and fully hydrated before you perform a slap-and-fold.)

1. To perform a slap-and-fold, pour the dough out onto a clean countertop.
2. Scoop your hands under the middle of the dough from the top and bottom (vertically) (see image 1).
3. Lift the dough up into the air, rotating your hands (see image 2).
4. Slap the dough down onto the countertop. As you slap the dough down, fold the dough's lifted part over itself and away from you (see image 3).
5. Repeat this process for several minutes or until you notice the dough starting to come together and appearing less shaggy. Return the dough to the bowl, cover, and proceed as per the recipe.

1

2

3

Lamination

Lamination is a technique that can develop gluten very effectively. It can also be used to evenly incorporate inclusions into a loaf of sourdough bread. The dough is gently stretched into a thin sheet and folded onto itself to enhance the dough's elasticity. Lamination is performed during bulk fermentation, typically after the first stretch-and-fold.

1. To perform a lamination, pour your dough out onto a clean countertop.
2. Using lightly moistened hands, from the middle of the dough, gently stretch the dough outward, moving around the dough. Continue pulling outward until the dough is as thin as it can be without tearing (see image 1). (The dough may appear almost translucent in spots.)
3. Fold the stretched dough in thirds (see image 2).
4. Roll it up from the bottom (see image 3). Return the dough to the bowl, cover, and proceed as per the recipe.

Understanding Proofing

One of the biggest challenges that people new to sourdough baking encounter is understanding proofing. This section will help you to attain a better grasp of the terminology, proofing process, factors that can influence proofing time, and how to tell when your dough is ready to be shaped and baked.

What Is Proofing?

Proofing is the process by which, over the passage of time, the dough ferments and gluten develops. Fermentation occurs when sourdough yeast and bacteria feed on the simple carbohydrates contained in the dough, which then produces carbon dioxide and ethanol. The fermentation process allows the dough to develop flavor, structure, and volume.

The Proofing Phases

There are three different phases of proofing: bulk proof, cold proof, and final proof (though not all recipes will use all three phases).

Bulk proof: The bulk proof is the first rise, when the dough is proofing in a singular mass at room temperature, and before the dough has been divided and shaped. During this phase, most of the carbon dioxide production occurs, giving rise to your dough. In some sourdough breads, the end of the bulk proof is followed by shaping of the dough and then a cold proof. In most enriched sourdough breads, the dough is placed in the refrigerator *en masse*, and then shaped after the cold proof.

Cold proof: The cold proof *sometimes* follows the bulk proof, in which time in the refrigerator is required to help develop the flavor of the dough and make it easier to handle. During a cold proof, the bacteria in the dough produce acids that can enhance the flavor profile of the dough. Chilled dough is also firmer and less sticky, which simplifies the shaping process when making enriched doughs. Making sourdough is a long process, and a cold proof may also allow for the prolonged process to be divided over 2 days.

Final proof: In a basic sourdough loaf, the cold proof is the final proof. However, for enriched doughs and buns, there is a final proof where the dough is degassed, divided, shaped into the requisite shape and then proofed again at room temperature (or in a controlled temperature environment like a proofing box or drawer). The degassing helps to redistribute and reactivate the yeast and allows for a more even crumb structure to develop.

Factors That Affect Proofing

There are a number of factors that can have an impact on the proofing of your dough.

Temperature: Temperature is one of the most impactful factors that can influence fermentation. Warmer temperatures result in faster proofing; whereas, cooler temperatures slow it down. If I am proofing at room temperature as opposed to in a controlled environment, like a proofing box, I may have to adjust my proofing schedule depending on how warm or cool the ambient room temperature is. In the winter, when I keep my thermostat set to 66°F (19°C), my basic sourdough loaf may bulk ferment for ten or more hours. Whereas in the summer, when I keep my thermostat set to 74°F (23°C), it may take only 6 hours! Moreover, if I decide to use cold ingredients, the cooler temperature of the dough results in slower fermentation.

As a result, you may have to adjust the duration of proofing to account for the differences in ambient room and dough temperatures.

In summary: warmer temperatures equal faster fermentation; colder temperatures equal slower fermentation.

Hydration: The higher the water content in the dough or the higher the hydration, the faster the dough will ferment. The reason for faster fermentation is that increased water increases the mobility of the enzymes in the dough, more easily breaking down the starches that the yeast and bacteria feed upon.

The higher the hydration, the more easily yeast can produce carbon dioxide. Moreover, as you likely know, bacteria thrive in wetter environments, and therefore are able to more quickly produce lactic acid and acetic acid, which are necessary byproducts of adequate fermentation.

In summary: higher-hydration doughs equal faster fermentation; lower-hydration doughs equal slower fermentation.

Elevation: High altitudes mean lower air pressure, which leads to faster fermentation. This may be due to the reduced carbon dioxide during fermentation at high altitudes. (Carbon dioxide can inhibit yeast metabolism.) If you are making sourdough at elevations greater than 3,000 feet (914m), you may notice a faster fermentation rate than under otherwise similar conditions at a lower elevation.

In summary: higher elevation equals faster fermentation; lower elevation equals slower fermentation.

Starter: Your dough will ferment faster with a higher percentage of starter. The reason for this is simple: As you introduce more bacteria and yeast to your dough, the faster the nutrients will be consumed by said microorganisms.

In summary: more starter equals faster fermentation; less starter equals slower fermentation.

Flour type: The flour that you use can greatly impact the flavor, volume, color, texture, and fermentation rate. Due to the increased nutrients available to the yeast and bacteria in whole grain flours (in particular wheat bran and wheat germ), your dough is likely to ferment a lot faster than with all white flours.

In summary: whole grain flour equals faster fermentation; all white flours equal slower fermentation.

Other ingredients: Certain ingredients can slow fermentation immensely, and it is important to either account for that when first adding these ingredients or consider adding them toward the end of bulk fermentation. When using cinnamon or raw garlic, I try to add these toward the end of bulk fermentation as the antimicrobial properties of both can inhibit fermentation.

When making enriched doughs with added fat (butter, oils) and sugar, you may notice fermentation slows significantly. Whereas a nonenriched dough may take just 6 hours to double in size, an enriched dough fermenting at the same temperature may take nearly double that amount of time. To account for this, I try to proof enriched doughs in a warmer environment, either in my proofing box or in the oven with the oven light on.

In summary: the addition of cinnamon, raw garlic, fats, or sugars can result in slower fermentation.

Knowing When Your Dough Is Well-Proofed

One of the most important things to remember about making sourdough is to watch the dough and not the clock. Most of my recipes recommend letting the dough double prior to a cold proof. The timing to reach this point will vary depending on the factors listed above, but the ambient room and dough temperatures are the most impactful factors affecting the timing of proofing.

Here are some cues that will provide information on whether your dough is well proofed.

Rise: During fermentation, your dough will rise (increase in volume). Most of my recipes advise to let the dough double in volume before a cold proof. This may need to be adjusted, because if you are in a very warm environment (say over 79°F [26°C]), your dough will take a lot longer to cool in the fridge than dough that has been proofed at 66°F (19°C). While the dough temperature drops, it will continue to proof.

Bubbles: If you proof your dough in a clear glass bowl and look at the underside of the dough, you will notice fermentation activity in the appearance of bubbles. You may also notice bubbles forming on the top of the dough. With underproofed doughs, you will notice less aeration of the dough; with overproofed doughs, you may notice many large bubbles dispersed throughout the dough.

Dough handling: With the exception of high-hydration doughs, a dough that is properly proofed will be easy to shape. Underproofed doughs can often be sticky and firm, whereas overproofed doughs will be extremely sticky, adhering to your hands and the countertop surface.

Finger-poke test: The finger-poke test is performed after the dough has been shaped, the second proofing is complete, and just prior to baking to determine whether the dough is ready to be baked. I use the finger-poke test prior to baking all my breads, including my basic loaves, buns, baguettes, and enriched doughs.

To perform the finger-poke test, gently press a floured finger into the top of the dough about ½-inch (1.25cm) deep. If the dough fills back in or springs back, it is underproofed; if the dough fills in slowly to the halfway point, it is ready to bake. If it does not fill in at all, it is overproofed.

Jiggliness: For lack of a better term, I determine that an enriched dough is ready to bake by its "jiggliness," or how much it wobbles when I shake the pan. Like the finger-poke test, this test is performed after the dough has been shaped, the second proofing is complete, and just prior to baking. This method is only accurate for doughs that have been shaped into forms that have rounded edges on the bottom (like croissants or rolls). For all other shapes, I continue to perform the finger-poke test.

How to tell if your dough is underproofed, well-proofed, or overproofed:

Factor	*Underproofed*	*Well-proofed*	*Overproofed*
Texture when shaping	Stiff, resistant to stretching	Pliable, smooth, easy to handle	Slack, overly relaxed, prone to tearing when stretched; will not hold shape
Stickiness	Slightly tacky	Slightly tacky but manageable	Very sticky, adheres to hands and work surface
Volume	Little rise	Doubled in volume	Overly expanded, puffy, more than doubled in volume
Surface tension	Smooth and taut, minimal bounce	Smooth and taut, bouncy	Loose, wrinkly, possibly deflated
Finger-poke test	Springs back quickly	Springs back slowly and only fills the indentation partway	Does not spring back, leaves an indentation
Oven spring	Unpredictable; depending on how underproofed, may get very little rise or a lot of rise and oven spring with a large belly	Controlled and even, no overexpanded belly	Minimal or none
Crumb structure	Uneven crumb and uneven distribution of air pockets (alveoli), areas of very small alveoli, and other areas with large alveoli	Even distribution of alveoli throughout the dough; rounded alveoli	Denser, evenly distributed alveoli; alveoli appear drooped or saggy
Flavor	Mild, possibly bland	Balanced and slightly tangy	More sour profile due to excess acid
Mouthfeel	Gummy, dense	Light but chewy	Dense

Overproofed
Well-proofed
Underproofed

Even crumb, but drooped or saggy alveoli
Even crumb, rounded alveoli
Uneven crumb, areas of very small alveoli and other areas of large alveoli
Overproofed
Well-proofed
Underproofed

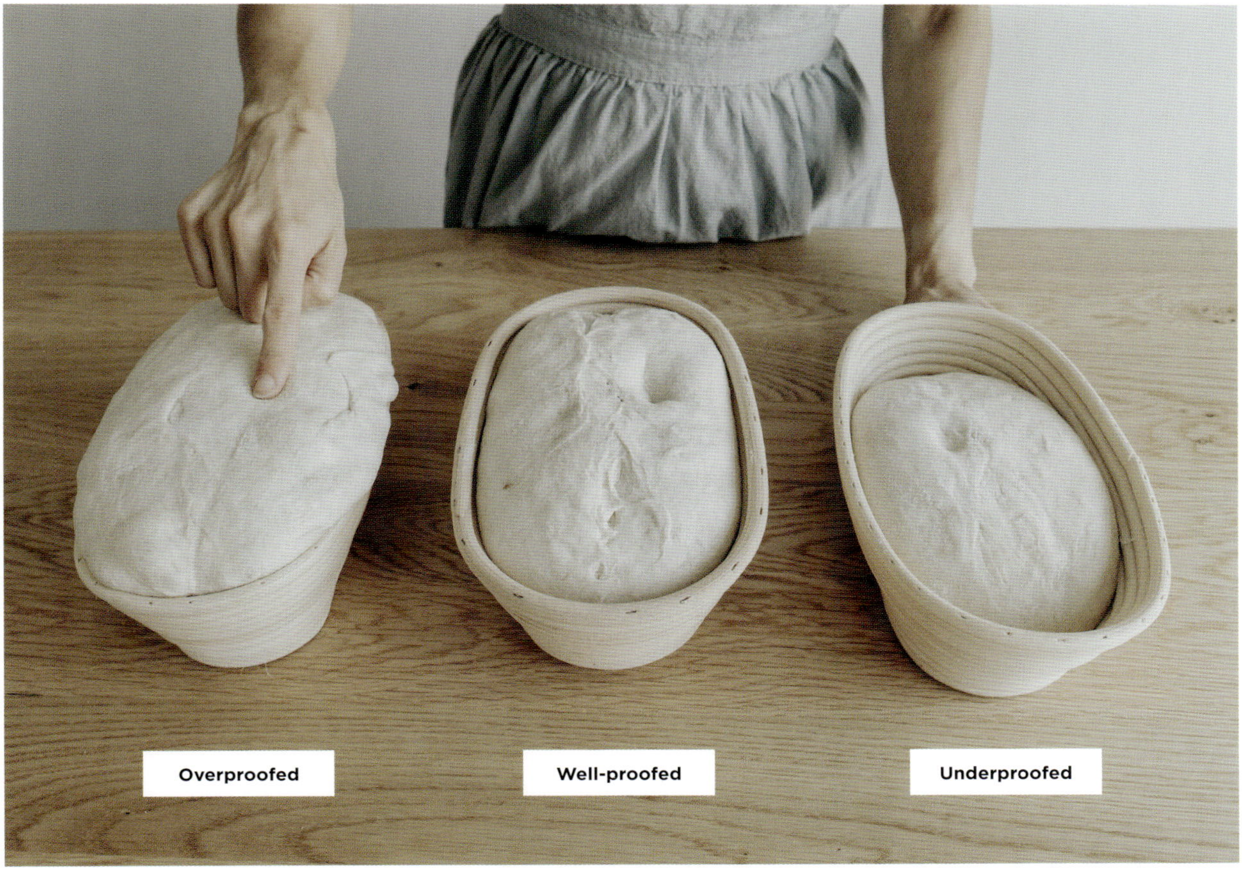

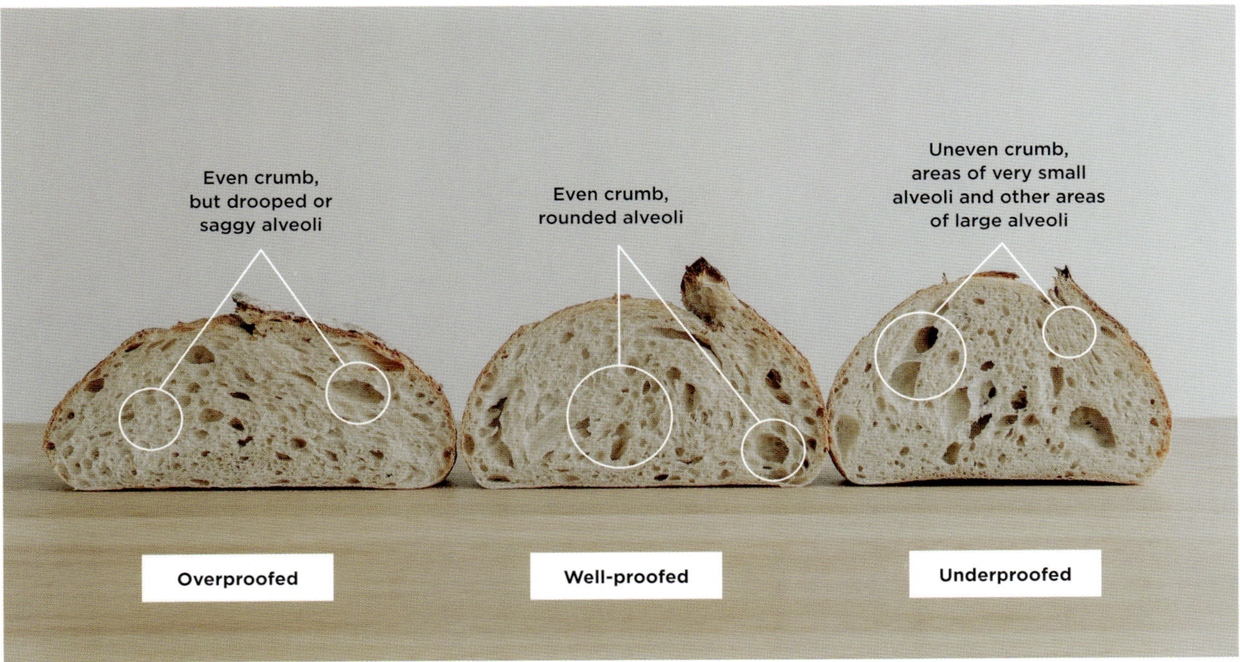

Frequently Asked Questions about Proofing

Proofing can be one of the trickiest parts of sourdough baking. If your dough isn't behaving as expected, don't worry—there are a few common issues and most are easy to address. From the strength of your starter to the temperature or altitude of your home, this section walks you through potential issues and how to fix them.

Why Did My Sourdough Not Rise During Proofing?

There are a number of factors that could contribute to the lack of rise during proofing.

First, look at your starter:

- How young is your starter? If it's very young, it's possible you'll need to continue with the daily feeding regime until you see it doubling in size. If it's a starter you have used successfully before, it's possible you'll need to strengthen your starter through more frequent feeding.
- Did you use the starter when it was at peak? If you used it before it peaked, it will take a lot longer for it to proof dough. The same is true if you use a starter that has fallen and has few bubbles remaining. And while you still *can* use starter at these points, it can produce more inconsistent results. Ensuring you have a healthy, active starter prior to making the dough can ensure a consistent rise.

Next, examine your environment:

- Do you live in a very cold climate or is your ambient room temperature less than 70°F (21°C)? If so, it's possible your dough has not had enough time to fully proof. If this is the case, let your dough sit for a longer period of time at room temperature.
- Do you live at a low altitude or have you recently moved from a high altitude to a low altitude? If so, dough will take longer to proof. It has been shown that dough will proof slower at lower elevations due to the increased atmospheric pressure on the dough, resisting the expansion of carbon dioxide that the yeast produces during fermentation.

Your environment can greatly impact the speed at which your dough rises. You may have to make adjustments to the timing of the recipes to ensure an adequately proofed dough!

Why Is My Dough So Sticky?

A number of factors can affect the consistency of the dough.

Proofing: A dough that has been overproofed (fermented too long) can be extremely sticky, as the gluten has started to break down and no longer provides structure to the dough. A dough that is very underproofed might also be a little sticky to the touch. And while the gluten may not have started breaking down, the lack of adequate fermentation, which contributes to the gluten formation and dough structure, may result in a slightly stickier dough.

Hydration and flours: I love high hydration doughs. I find they produce fluffier, moister breads. That being said, sometimes a flour might not be able to handle the amount of water that a recipe calls for. Some factors that can affect the absorptive quality of flour:

- **Protein:** Flours that contain a higher amount of protein are better able to absorb water. This is due to the fact that the protein molecules bind to the water to create gluten, thus improving the dough structure. A high-protein flour is typically anything above 12%.
- **Flour type:** Whole-grain flours are also able to better absorb water due to the presence of bran and germ (unlike just the endosperm present in refined flour).
- **Ash content:** Higher ash content equals higher water absorption.
- **Flour consistency:** Coarse flour equals lower absorption.
- **Ambient humidity:** Flour stored in a humid environment is less absorptive, while flour stored in a dry environment is more absorptive.

If your dough is too sticky upon shaping, you can dust it with all-purpose flour. However, if you think your dough might be overproofed, see below.

What Causes Overproofing?

Overproofing is caused by proofing the dough too long, resulting in a breakdown in gluten and therefore the structure of the dough, producing a slack and nonelastic dough.

Can You Rescue an Overproofed Dough?

While overproofed dough can't be returned to a well-proofed state, there are methods to recover it enough to bake successfully. Pour the dough out onto your shaping surface, degas it (press and fold the dough to remove the air), reshape it and place it back

into the banneton (or whatever equipment you're using to store the dough). Proof it at room temperature until a finger-poke test reveals a slow return of the dough.

How Long Does It Take to Proof the Bread?

Duration of proofing depends on the environment in which the dough is proofed.

Why Do You Do a Cold/Refrigerator Proof for Most of Your Recipes?

Sourdough can take a long time to create, and performing a cold proof (a.k.a. a cold ferment or cold retard) can help to break up the process and allow you time to rest. It can also enhance the flavor profile and texture of the bread. For enriched high-hydration doughs, cold proofing also makes the dough easier to handle when shaping for the final proof.

Do I Have to Do a Cold/Refrigerator Proof?

It is not required; however, it can positively impact the flavor of the bread, creating a more sour profile. If you decide not to do a cold proof, you will need to proof it longer at room temperature after shaping. You'll want to proof it at room temperature until a finger-poke reveals a slow return of the dough.

How Long Can I Cold Proof My Dough?

For my basic loaf, I have successfully cold proofed my sourdough for 3 days. Beyond this, I find the dough becomes overproofed with minimal oven spring and poor structure.

My Loaf Came Out Gummy. How Can I Prevent That from Happening?

Several factors can contribute to a gummy loaf:

- A dough in which an inactive starter has been used can contribute to poor proofing, producing a gummy loaf.
- Underbaking a loaf might result in a gummy interior. Ensure you are baking your loaves until they are the desired internal temperature. For my basic sourdough bread, I always knock on the bottom of the loaf—a hollow sound means the dough is ready to be removed from the oven.
- An inadequately cooled loaf may also be gummy in texture. Ensure you're completely cooling your loaves before slicing. (Believe me, I *understand* the temptation to slice into a warm loaf of bread, but this can impact the overall texture of the loaf!)

How Do I Get More and Bigger Holes and a More Open Crumb in My Bread?

While I understand the desire to produce a more open crumb for an "Instagram-worthy" photo, it is not the hallmark of a good loaf of sourdough bread! That being said, here are some tips to help achieve a more open crumb:

- Ensure the hydration is between 75% and 85%.
- Use a high-protein flour that is at least 12%.
- Ensure adequate gluten development using techniques like autolyse (p. 32) and lamination (p. 37).
- Ensure proper fermentation: An underproofed dough will produce a variable crumb some large alveoli and then dense pockets with smaller holes. An overproofed dough will produce a more even crumb, but as it loses gluten structure, it will not be able to rise as well.

How Can I Make My Sourdough More Sour or Less Sour?

Several factors contribute to the sourness of a bread, including the starter, the fermentation, and the type of flour used in the bread.

Starter:

- *A starter that is fed a 1:1:1 ratio will produce a milder, less sour bread.* A starter fed at this ratio ferments faster, favoring yeast activity versus lactic and acetic acid bacteria activity. Lactic and acetic acid bacteria, which produce a more sour profile, require more time for the acids to accumulate. Conversely, a starter fed at a ratio of 1:5:5, for example, will require a longer time to reach peak, which favors production of acids (lactic and acetic) by the bacteria. (Note: A starter fed 1:1:1 ratio requires more frequent feedings to prevent overacidification. If it is not fed frequently, it will produce a more sour bread.)
- *A starter that is stiffer (around 50% to 60% hydration) will produce a milder, less sour bread.* Stiff starters favor yeast activity over bacterial, resulting in a milder flavor and fewer sour notes. It should be mentioned that while stiff starters do favor production of acetic acid, which is typically more sour than lactic acid, yeast is able to better tolerate the lower hydration environment. This leads to increased yeast growth and activity, which can mask the sour profile of the acetic acid. (Note: A stiff starter can produce a sour bread if it is fermented in cool temperatures, which favors production of acetic acid.)
- *A starter that is used at peak will produce a milder, less sour bread.* A starter at peak has a high presence of yeast fermentative activity. Bacteria are present but have not yet produced as much acid. A fallen starter has fermented more, resulting in increased production of acids from the bacteria, producing a more sour profile.
- *More starter used in your recipe will produce a milder, less sour bread, similar to the concept above.* A higher ratio of starter favors yeast versus lactic acid bacteria activity, producing a milder flavor profile.

Fermentation:

- *A shorter fermentation time will produce a milder, less sour bread.* I am not referring to underfermenting, but rather, placing the dough in a warmer environment to help speed up fermentation. Shorter fermentation favors yeast activity and gives the bacteria less time to accumulate.
- *Warmer environments (75°F to 82°F [24°C to 28°C]) will produce a milder, less sour bread.* Warmer temperatures favor production of yeast and lactic acid bacteria, both of which produce a milder flavor. Conversely, cooler temperatures (60°F to 72°F [15°C to 22°C]) favor production of acetic acid, which has a more sour profile.
- *Cold proofing your dough may increase the sour profile of your bread.* Placing the dough in the refrigerator for an extended period of time (12 to 36 hours) may produce a more sour profile due to the increased production of acetic acid and decreasing activity of yeast.

Flour:

- *A dough using whole grains will produce a more sour bread.* The bran from whole-grain flours has a buffering capacity, which means that it can resist changes in pH, producing a more pronounced sour profile due to increased production of lactic and acetic acids during proofing. Rye flour in particular promotes production of acetic acid, which makes the bread noticeably more sour.

Shaping Sourdough

Though not necessary, shaping sourdough is an important part of making a loaf. While you could certainly just pour the dough out of the bowl and into a pan and bake it, there are several reasons why shaping the dough can improve a loaf.

- **Structural integrity:** Shaping helps to provide much-needed structural integrity to a loaf. It creates surface tension, which allows the loaf to bloom in the oven, and will help provide the best "oven spring" or rise.
- **Even crumb:** Shaping helps to redistribute the bubbles that have developed in your bread, providing a more even crumb.
- **Crust texture:** By creating surface tension on the loaf during shaping, you can enhance the crust's texture. A tighter outer surface leads to more uniform caramelization of the crust during baking.
- **Aesthetics:** Shaping a loaf determines how it will look after it is baked (boule, batard, loaf pan-shaped, etc.). Many bakers see success in sourdough through the formation of an "ear"—a ridge or flap of crust that forms along the scoring line of a loaf of bread. The ear cannot be achieved without proper shaping. Shaping also allows you to easily decorate a loaf of bread.

With these points in mind, I will walk you through the steps required to shape a boule and a batard, the two most common shapes of freeform (not in a pan) sourdough bread.

Shaping a Batard

A batard is an oval-shaped loaf of sourdough bread. Some people prefer shaping batards because they provide more evenly sized slices that are perfect for sandwiches. There are many ways to shape a batard, this is just one method I find provides the most consistent result and with excellent surface tension.

Once you have preshaped your loaf and allowed it to rest, follow these instructions to shape a batard:

1. Lightly flour a clean countertop or lightly dampen it with water. Turn the dough seam-side up and with either lightly dampened or lightly floured fingers, gently press the dough into a rectangle, with the long side facing you. You do not want to fully degas the dough, so it is important that you use a gentle hand (see image 1).
2. Letterfold the dough by taking the two corners of one short side and bringing them to the two-thirds point of the dough. Take the other two corners on the other short side and bring them on top of the dough you just folded (see image 2).
3. Grasp the dough from the (now) short side facing you and tuck and roll the dough while gently pulling to create surface tension until you have rolled it all the way up (see image 3).
4. Dust the top (smooth side) of the dough with rice flour, place it seam-side up into the banneton, and proceed with your recipe (see image 4).

1
2
3
4

1
2
3
4

Shaping a Boule

A boule is a round loaf of sourdough bread. Boules can make for an easier canvas on which to create a symmetrical score or decoration. They are also more rustic and traditional in appearance.

Once you have shaped your loaf and allowed it to rest, follow these instructions to shape a boule:

1. Lightly flour a clean countertop or lightly dampen it with water. Turn the dough seam-side up and with either lightly dampened or lightly floured fingers, gently press the dough into a circle (see image 1).
2. Grasp an edge of the dough using your thumb and index/middle fingers and fold it into the center. Move to the opposite edge of the dough and fold it to the center (see image 2).
3. Repeat with the other two edges. At this point, you should have four "sides" that have been brought to the middle of the dough, and four "corners" of the dough (see image 3).
4. Flip the dough seam-side down (smooth-side up) and with a bench scraper or your hands, pull the dough gently toward you to tighten the surface. Rotate the dough slightly and repeat, using gentle pressure and keeping the shape round. Continue until the surface is smooth and taut (see image 4).
5. Dust the top (smooth side) of the dough with rice flour. Place it seam-side up into the banneton and proceed with your recipe (see image 5).

CHAPTER 3

Basic Sourdough Loaves

Total time: about 36 hours
Active prep time: 1–1½ hours
Baking time: 40–50 minutes
Makes: 2 loaves

SPECIAL EQUIPMENT

Dutch oven/bread cloche (I use a Fourneau Grande)
Banneton (optional)
Bread lame (optional)

INGREDIENTS

720g room-temperature tap water
200g active 100%-hydration sourdough starter
20g sea salt
850g white bread flour
150g einkorn, spelt, or whole wheat flour

Sourdough Enzo Master Loaf

While many bakers profess the complexity of making sourdough bread, it can be as simple or as challenging as you want it to be. For me, making sourdough has grown into so much more than just baking—it's a passion, a creative outlet, and a form of therapy. There's comfort and peace in the slow process, and then deep satisfaction in pulling a warm loaf from the oven that you created with time and care.

This is the recipe I have returned to for several years—the one that helped me understand the nuances of certain practices like autolyse, slap-and-fold, and lamination (all methods of developing gluten; see chapter 2 *Gluten Development, Proofing, and Shaping* for explanations of each). However, if your bread flour has a protein content of 12.5 percent or higher, you can avoid these added (and slightly more complex) steps and still achieve a beautiful loaf.

This is my master recipe—a straightforward, medium-hydration loaf made with a 100%-hydration peaked sourdough starter and a blend of flours that bring both strength and flavor to the dough. (See *Making Your Own Sourdough Starter* on page 16.)

Make and proof the dough (30 minutes active, 4–10 hours bulk proof at room temperature)

1. To a large mixing bowl, add the water and starter. Mix well with a fork until fully combined.
2. Add the salt and stir to combine.
3. Add the flours and mix by hand or with a dough whisk until you have a shaggy dough. Cover with plastic wrap or a reusable bowl cover and let the dough rest for 30 to 45 minutes.
4. After the allotted time has passed, wet your hands with water and perform a stretch-and-fold (p. 34). Cover and let the dough rest for 30 to 45 minutes.
5. After the allotted time has passed, wet your hands again and perform your first coil fold (p. 35). Cover and let the dough rest for 45 to 60 minutes.
6. Perform three more coil folds as above with 45- to 60-minute intervals in between each fold, covering the dough each time. (Once you have completed the final coil fold, the dough will feel tight, will not stretch as easily, nor will it break when you do the coil fold.)
7. Allow the dough to rest, covered, until it has almost doubled in size. (Note that the amount of time it will take for the dough to almost double in size will vary depending on a number of factors, but primarily the ambient room temperature of your kitchen. If it is cooler in your home, say 64°F to 66°F (18°C to 19°C), it could take as long as an additional 6 hours to reach this point; if it is warmer 75°F to 77°F (24°C to 25°C), it may only take an additional 2 or 3 hours!)

Shape the dough (5 minutes active, 60–90 minutes rest, overnight cold proof)

1. Pour the dough out onto a lightly floured surface. To start preshaping the dough, divide the dough into two equal-size pieces using a bench scraper. Use wet fingers to knock back the larger air bubbles by lightly pressing into the dough. (This helps to redistribute the air throughout the dough for a more even crumb.) Pull the edges of the dough into the middle to create a ball, then flip the dough smooth-side up and use the surface of the counter to create tension on the dough by pulling it toward you. Let the dough rest uncovered on the counter for 30 to 60 minutes.

2. Follow the dough-shaping instructions for making a boule (p. 49) or a batard (p. 46). Place the shaped dough into a linen-lined bowl or banneton of your choice and let it rest for 30 minutes. Cover the dough with a bowl cover and place it in the refrigerator overnight. (Note: The dough can safely remain in the refrigerator for up to 72 hours—however, beyond this point, the dough can become overproofed.)

Score and bake the bread (10–20 minutes active, 1 hour freezer [optional], 50 minutes bake)

1. When you are ready to bake, place your covered banneton in the freezer for 1 hour if you plan to do a decorative score. Place a bread cloche in the oven and preheat it to 490°F (255°C). If you do not plan to do a decorative score, simply preheat your oven with the cast-iron cloche inside.
2. Turn out the dough onto a piece of parchment paper or a dough sling and complete your decorative score. Place the dough in the cloche, covered, for 7 minutes, then remove the dough from the oven and complete your expansion score (p. 219). If you have done a decorative score, do not inoculate the cloche with steam. Adding water or ice into the cloche will result in the design being steamed off. If you have not done a decorative score, you may inoculate with steam by adding 2 to 3 ice cubes to the cloche.
3. Place the dough back in the oven for 20 to 25 minutes, covered. Then remove the cover and bake for an additional 10 to 15 minutes. The bread should sound hollow when knocked on the bottom or have an internal temperature of 195°F (91°C). If the loaf does not sound hollow, place it back in the oven for 10 minutes.
4. Remove the loaf from the oven and place it on a cooling rack for 1 hour before slicing. Store the bread at room temperature in a resealable bag for 3 days or freeze for up to 2 months in an airtight container or freezer bag.

Total time: 36 hours
Active prep time: 30–40 minutes
Baking time: 45–55 minutes
Makes: 1 loaf

EQUIPMENT

Stand mixer fitted with dough hook (optional)
Dutch oven/bread cloche (I use a Fourneau Grande)
Banneton (optional)
Bread lame (optional)

INGREDIENTS

390g tap water
100g active 100%-hydration sourdough starter
10g sea salt
500g whole wheat flour

Sourdough Enzo Whole Wheat Loaf

This 100-percent whole wheat loaf is a hearty departure from my usual bakes, which often lean on bread flour for softness and structure. With its denser crumb and satisfying chew, this loaf highlights the nutty flavor of whole wheat with every bite. Enjoy this bread with a generous slab of butter and a drizzle of honey, or stack it high with your favorite sandwich fixings.

Prepare and proof the dough (15 minutes active, 3–10 hours bulk proof at room temperature)

1. In a medium bowl or the bowl of a stand mixer, combine the water, starter, salt, and whole wheat flour. Knead on low or mix by hand until the ingredients are incorporated. Cover the dough with a bowl cover or plastic wrap and let it rest for 30 to 45 minutes.
2. Perform a stretch-and-fold (p. 34). Cover and let the dough rest for another 30 to 45 minutes.
3. After the allotted time has elapsed, perform a coil fold (p. 35). Cover and let the dough rest for 30 to 45 minutes more.
4. Perform two more coil folds over the next 2 hours. Cover and let the dough rest until airy and not quite doubled in size. This may take 3 to 10 hours, depending on the ambient room temperatures. (The higher percentage of whole grains means that this loaf is not going to achieve as much rise as an all-white loaf.)

Shape the dough (5 minutes active, overnight cold proof)

1. Pour the dough out onto a clean countertop and shape into desired loaf shape. (See chapter 2 *Gluten Development, Proofing, and Shaping* for shaping options.) Place it into a linen-lined bowl or banneton of your choice.
2. Cover and let the dough sit at room temperature for 30 minutes. Place the covered dough in the refrigerator for an overnight cold proof.

Bake and store the loaf (10–20 minutes active, 1 hour freezer [optional], 45–55 minutes bake)

1. In the morning, place a bread cloche inside the oven and preheat to 450°F (230°C). If you plan to do a decorative score, place the dough in the freezer for 1 hour prior to baking.
2. Turn the dough out onto a piece of parchment paper or a dough sling and complete your decorative score, if you plan to. Score the dough with your bread lame or a very sharp knife. If you have done a decorative score, bake the dough for 7 minutes and then perform the expansion score (p. 219).
3. Bake the dough in the bread cloche for 30 minutes covered, then uncover and bake for an additional 15 minutes. Knock the bottom of the loaf and if it sounds hollow and the internal temperature has reached 205°F to 210°F (96°C to 99°C), it is fully baked. If the loaf does not sound hollow, place it back in the oven for 10 minutes.
4. Let the bread cool on a wire rack for at least 1 hour before slicing.
5. Store at room temperature in a resealable bag for 3 days or freeze in an airtight container or freezer bag for up to 2 months.

Total time: 36 hours
Active prep time: 30–40 minutes
Baking time: 45–55 minutes
Makes: 1 loaf

SPECIAL EQUIPMENT

Stand mixer fitted with dough hook (optional)
Dutch oven/bread cloche (I use a Fourneau Grande)
Banneton (optional)
Bread lame (optional)

INGREDIENTS

390g tap water
100g active 100%-hydration sourdough starter
10g sea salt
350g white bread flour
150g dark rye flour

Rye-Blend Loaf

This hearty, 30 percent-rye loaf strikes a beautiful balance between the glutinous, more open structure of bread flour with the earthy aroma of rye. It is denser than my master loaf and with a slightly tighter crumb, but it has added fiber and a complex flavor thanks to the higher percentage of whole grains. This loaf will become a fast favorite in your recipe repertoire!

Prepare and proof the dough (15 minutes active, 3–10 hours bulk proof at room temperature)

1. In a medium bowl or the bowl of a stand mixer, combine the water, starter, salt, bread flour, and rye flour. Knead on low or mix by hand until the ingredients are incorporated. Cover the dough with a bowl cover or plastic wrap and let it rest for 30 to 45 minutes.
2. Perform a stretch-and-fold (p. 34). Cover and let the dough rest for another 30 to 45 minutes.
3. After the allotted time has elapsed, perform a coil fold (p. 35). Cover and let the dough rest for another 30 to 45 minutes.
4. Perform two more coil folds over the next 2 hours. Cover and let the dough rest until airy and not quite doubled in size. This may take 3 to 10 hours, depending on ambient room temperature. (The higher percentage of whole grains means that this loaf is not going to achieve as much rise as an all-white loaf.)

Shape the dough (5 minutes active, overnight cold proof)

1. Pour the dough out onto a clean countertop and shape into desired loaf shape. (See chapter 2 *Gluten Development, Proofing, and Shaping* for shaping options.) Place it into a linen-lined bowl or banneton of your choice.
2. Cover and let the dough sit at room temperature for 30 minutes. Place the covered dough into the refrigerator for an overnight cold proof.

Bake and store the loaf (10–20 minutes active, 1 hour freezer [optional], 45–55 minutes bake)

1. In the morning, place a bread cloche inside the oven and preheat to 450°F (230°C). If you plan to do a decorative score, place the dough in the freezer for 1 hour before scoring.
2. Turn the dough out onto a piece of parchment paper or a dough sling and complete your decorative score, if you plan to. Score the dough with your bread lame or a very sharp knife. If you have done a decorative score, bake the dough for 7 minutes, then perform the expansion score (p. 217).
3. Bake the dough in the bread cloche for 30 minutes covered, then uncover and bake for an additional 15 minutes. Knock the bottom of the loaf, and if it sounds hollow and the internal temperature reaches 205°F to 210°F (96°C to 99°C), it is fully baked. If the loaf does not sound hollow, place it back in the oven for 10 minutes to ensure it is baked fully.
4. Let the bread cool on a wire rack for at least 1 hour before slicing.
5. Store at room temperature in a resealable bag for 3 days or freeze in an airtight container or freezer bag for up to 2 months.

Total time: 28 hours
Active prep time: 20 minutes
Baking time: 1 hour
Makes: 1 loaf

EQUIPMENT

Stand mixer
One 8.5 × 4.75 × 4.375-inch (22 × 12 × 11cm) Pullman loaf pan

INGREDIENTS

Seed soaker

185g rye berries
70g raw, hulled sunflower seeds
65g raw, hulled pumpkin seeds
35g flaxseeds

Levain

65g tap water
15g 100%-hydration sourdough starter
65g dark rye flour

Dough

165g plus 35g dark rye flour
165g plus 35g bread flour
175g tap water
All of the prepared levain
Drained seed soaker
55g fancy (light) molasses
13g sea salt

Rugbrød

Rugbrød is a Danish rye bread that is known for its unique texture, density, and deep flavor. While it doesn't have a typical bread texture, what it lacks in gluten is made up for in its richness and complexity. This is my sourdough spin on the traditional loaf, using a rye-flour levain to enhance the depth of flavor. This loaf is as nourishing as it is delicious.

Prepare the seed soaker and levain (10 minutes)

1. The evening before mixing the dough, prepare the seed soaker by mixing all seeds together in a wide, shallow bowl. Add enough water to ensure the seeds are fully covered.
2. Cover the seed soaker with a bowl cover or plastic wrap and let it sit at room temperature overnight.
3. Once the seed soaker is covered, prepare the levain by mixing all the levain ingredients in a 1-liter (34fl oz) jar. Cover the jar with plastic wrap and set aside to rise overnight at room temperature.

Make the dough (10 minutes, 4–10 hours room-temperature proof, and another 2–6 hours room-temperature proof)

1. The next morning, once the levain has fully risen, make the dough by mixing together 165 grams dark rye flour and 165 grams bread flour, along with the water and levain until fully combined. (There is no need to knead the dough. It will form a shaggy, wet dough.) Cover and let the dough rise until doubled, about 4 to 10 hours.
2. Transfer the risen dough to the bowl of a stand mixer fitted with a paddle attachment. Pour off any water remaining in the seed soaker, then add the seed mix to the bowl along with the molasses, 35 grams rye flour, 35 grams bread flour, and salt. Mix for 2 to 3 minutes, scraping the bowl halfway through to ensure dough is mixed thoroughly. Transfer the dough to a greased Pullman loaf pan. Proof until the dough has risen to about 1 inch (2.5cm) below the top of the loaf tin, about 2 to 6 hours.

Bake and store the bread (1 hour)

1. Preheat the oven to 500°F (260°C). Place the Pullman loaf pan cover on the loaf pan and place the dough in the oven for 15 minutes. After 15 minutes, drop the oven temperature to 375°F (190°C). Bake for an additional 45 minutes or until the internal temperature of the loaf reaches 200°F (93°C).
2. Allow the loaf to cool for 2 to 3 hours on a wire rack. To allow the crumb to fully set and add more depth of flavor to the loaf, it is recommended (though not required) to place it in a zipper-lock bag for 24 hours before slicing.

CHAPTER 4

Inclusions

Total time: 36 hours
Active prep time: 30 minutes
Baking time: 45 minutes
Makes: 1 loaf

SPECIAL EQUIPMENT

Stand mixer fitted with a dough hook (optional)
Dutch oven/bread cloche (I use a Fourneau Grande)
Bread lame (optional)

INGREDIENTS

Dough

360g tap water
100g active 100%-hydration sourdough starter
10g sea salt
425g white bread flour
75g whole wheat flour

Inclusions

35g poppyseeds
15g lemon zest (zest from 3 lemons)
70g honey

Lemon Poppyseed Loaf

This aromatic loaf is perfect slathered with butter, drizzled in honey, and served alongside a cup of coffee. The delicate sweetness of honey, the bright flavor of lemon, and the nutty crunch of poppyseeds, along with the subtle tang of sourdough, creates a beautiful blend of flavors and textures. This loaf is sure to elevate any table and will become a breakfast staple in your household!

Prepare the dough (15 minutes active, 1.5 hours rest)

1. In a medium bowl or the bowl of a stand mixer, combine the water, starter, salt, bread flour, and whole wheat flour. Knead on low or mix by hand until the ingredients are fully incorporated. Cover the dough with a bowl cover or plastic wrap and let it rest for 30 to 45 minutes.
2. Perform a stretch-and-fold (p. 34). Cover and let the dough rest for another 30 to 45 minutes.

Mix in the inclusions (10 minutes active, 3–6 hours bulk proof at room temperature)

1. Add the inclusions to the dough and mix using the stand mixer or by hand until the inclusions are fully incorporated. Cover and let the dough rest for 1 hour.
2. Perform a coil fold (p. 35). Cover and let the dough rest for 45 to 60 minutes.
3. Perform another coil fold. Cover and let the dough rest until it has doubled in size and appears airy and light. This may take 3 to 6 hours, depending on the ambient room temperature.

Shape the dough (5 minutes active, 30 minutes rest, overnight cold proof)

1. Turn the dough out onto a clean countertop dusted lightly with flour and shape into desired loaf shape. (See Chapter 2 *Gluten Development, Proofing, and Shaping* for shaping options.) Place it into a linen-lined bowl or banneton of your choice.
2. Cover and let the dough sit at room temperature for 30 minutes. Place the covered dough into the refrigerator for an overnight cold proof.

Bake and store the loaf (45 minutes bake)

1. In the morning, place a bread cloche inside the oven and preheat to 425°F (220°C).
2. Turn the dough out onto a piece of parchment paper or a dough sling and score with a bread lame or a very sharp kitchen knife.
3. Bake the dough in the bread cloche for 35 minutes covered, then uncover and bake for an additional 10 minutes. Knock the bottom of the loaf and if it sounds hollow and the internal temperature reaches 195°F (91°C), it is fully baked. If the loaf does not sound hollow, place it back in the oven for 10 minutes to ensure it is baked fully.
4. Let the bread cool on a wire rack for at least 1 hour before slicing.
5. Store at room temperature in a resealable bag for up to 3 days or freeze in an airtight container or freezer bag for up to 2 months.

Total time: 36 hours
Active prep time: 30 minutes
Baking time: 35–45 minutes
Makes: 1 loaf

EQUIPMENT

Stand mixer fitted with a dough hook (optional)
Dutch oven/bread cloche (I use a Fourneau Grande)
Banneton or open-topped loaf pan
Bread lame (optional)

INGREDIENTS

Dough

280g tap water
100g active 100%-hydration sourdough starter
9g sea salt
325g bread flour
75g whole wheat flour

Inclusions

60g unsalted butter
60g flaxseed

Browned Butter and Flaxseed Loaf

This loaf combines the nutty richness of the browned butter with the wholesome flavor and crunch of flaxseeds. It's perfect for a hearty sandwich or toasted with some butter and honey. With a balanced flavor and a satisfying chew, it's a loaf you will keep coming back to.

Prepare and rest the dough (10 minutes active, 30–45 minute rest)

1. In a medium bowl or the bowl of a stand mixer, combine the water, starter, salt, bread flour, and whole wheat flour. Knead on low or mix by hand until the ingredients are incorporated. Cover the dough with a bowl cover or plastic wrap and let it rest for 30 to 45 minutes.

Prepare and mix in the inclusions (10 minutes active, 45–60 minute rest)

1. Place the flaxseeds in a small heat-proof bowl.
2. In a small pan over medium heat, melt the butter, cooking it until it turns medium brown and smells like caramel. Promptly remove the pan from the heat and pour the browned butter over the flaxseeds.
3. Using the stand mixer or by hand, mix the butter and flaxseed mixture into the dough until it is fully incorporated and cohesive. Cover and let the dough rest for 45 to 60 minutes.

Proof and shape the dough (20 minutes active, 3–6 hours bulk proof at room temperature, overnight cold proof)

1. After the set time has elapsed, perform a coil fold (p. 35). Cover and let the dough rest for 45 minutes to 1 hour.
2. Repeat two more coil folds at 45- to 60-minute intervals, covering the dough with plastic wrap or a bowl cover during the resting time.
3. Once the coil folds are complete, allow the dough to ferment until it is not quite doubled in size and jiggly when the bowl is shaken, about 3 to 6 hours depending on the ambient room temperature.
4. Pour the dough out onto a clean countertop and shape into desired loaf shape. (See chapter 2 *Gluten Development, Proofing, and Shaping* for shaping options.) Place it into a linen-lined bowl, banneton of your choice, or open-topped loaf pan.
5. Cover and let the dough sit at room temperature for 30 minutes. Place the covered dough into the refrigerator for an overnight cold proof.

Bake and store the loaf (35–45 minutes)

1. In the morning, preheat the oven to 490°F (255°C) with a covered bread cloche placed inside. If your dough was proofed in a banneton, turn it out onto a piece of parchment paper or a dough sling. If it was proofed in a loaf pan, leave it in the loaf pan.
2. Score the dough, if desired. (Scoring is not necessary as the enrichment with the butter will prevent the dough from bursting.) Place the dough in the bread cloche and reduce the temperature to 450°F (230°C). Bake the dough in a covered bread cloche for 25 minutes, then uncover and bake for an additional 10 minutes. Knock the bottom of the loaf and if it sounds hollow and the internal temperature has reached 205°F to 210°F (96°C to 99°C), it is fully baked. If the loaf does not sound hollow, place it back in the oven for 10 minutes to complete baking.
3. Let the bread cool on a wire rack for at least 1 hour before slicing.
4. Store at room temperature in a resealable bag for up to 3 days or freeze in an airtight container or freezer bag for up to 2 months.

Total time: 36 hours
Active prep time: 30 minutes
Baking time: 40 minutes
Makes: 1 loaf

SPECIAL EQUIPMENT

Stand mixer fitted with a dough hook (optional)
Dutch oven/bread cloche (I use a Fourneau Grande)
Banneton (optional)
Bread lame (optional)

INGREDIENTS

Dough

260g tap water
100g active 100%-hydration sourdough starter
50g maple syrup
10g sea salt
440g white bread flour

Inclusions

50g dry rolled oats, cooked according to package directions
2g ground cinnamon
1g cardamom powder

Maple Oat Porridge Loaf

My homemade sourdough coupled with hearty oat porridge, cinnamon, and cardamom is the perfect way to start your day. The oats add a creamy richness while keeping the crumb tender and moist, and the maple syrup adds that hint of sweetness to round out the flavor. The loaf sits at the intersection of nourishment and indulgence, which is why I find myself returning to it again and again.

Prepare and proof the dough (25 minutes active, 2 hours rest, 3–6 hours bulk proof at room temperature)

1. In a medium bowl or the bowl of a stand mixer, combine the water, starter, maple syrup, salt, and bread flour. Knead on low or mix by hand until the ingredients are incorporated. Cover the dough with a bowl cover or plastic wrap and let it rest for 30 to 45 minutes.
2. Add the cooked oats to the dough and, using your hands or in the bowl of a stand mixer, knead until thoroughly combined. Cover and let the dough rest for 45 minutes.
3. Add the cinnamon and the cardamom and fold into the dough. Cover and let the dough rest for another 30 minutes.
4. Perform a coil fold (p. 35). Cover the dough and let it rest for 1 hour.
5. Perform two more coil folds over 2 hours, ensuring the dough is covered during resting time. Let it rest at room temperature until doubled in size. This may take roughly 3 to 6 hours depending on the ambient room temperature.

Shape the dough (5 minutes active, 30 minutes rest, overnight cold proof)

1. Pour the dough out onto a clean countertop dusted lightly with flour and shape into desired loaf shape. (See Chapter 2 *Gluten Development, Proofing, and Shaping* for shaping options.) Place it into a linen-lined bowl or banneton of your choice.
2. Cover and let the dough sit at room temperature for 30 minutes. Place the covered dough into the refrigerator for an overnight cold proof.

Bake and store the loaf (40 minutes bake)

1. In the morning, place a bread cloche inside the oven and preheat to 450°F (230°C).
2. Turn the dough out onto a piece of parchment paper or a dough sling and score with a bread lame or a very sharp kitchen knife.
3. Bake the dough in the bread cloche for 30 minutes covered, then uncover and bake for an additional 10 minutes. Knock the bottom of the loaf and if it sounds hollow and the internal temperature reaches 195°F to 200°F (91°C to 93°C), it is fully baked. If the loaf does not sound hollow, place it back in the oven for 10 minutes to ensure it is fully baked.
4. Let the bread cool on a wire rack for at least 1 hour before slicing.
5. Store at room temperature in a resealable bag for up to 3 days or freeze in an airtight container or freezer bag for up to 2 months.

Total time: 36 hours
Active prep time: 30 minutes
Baking time: 35–45 minutes
Makes: 1 loaf

SPECIAL EQUIPMENT

Stand mixer fitted with a dough hook (optional)
Dutch oven/bread cloche (I use a Fourneau Grande)
Banneton (optional)
Bread lame (optional)

INGREDIENTS

Dough

280g tap water
100g active 100%-hydration sourdough starter
70g honey
9g sea salt
325g bread flour
75g whole wheat flour

Inclusions

80g candied ginger, cut into 3⁄16-inch (5mm) pieces
5–6 sprigs fresh thyme, stems removed

Candied Ginger and Thyme Loaf

This fragrant loaf is a joyous balance of sweet and savory. With a tender crumb and a hint of sweetness from the honey and ginger, this one has become a family favorite. It is the kind of loaf that is best enjoyed warm with a drizzle of honey and a cup of hot tea.

Prepare the dough (20 minutes active, 2 hours rest)

1. In a medium bowl or the bowl of a stand mixer, combine the water, starter, honey, salt, bread flour, and whole wheat flour. Knead on low or mix by hand until the ingredients are incorporated. Cover the dough with a bowl cover or plastic wrap and let it rest for 30 to 45 minutes.
2. Perform a stretch-and-fold (p. 34). Cover and let the dough rest for another 30 to 45 minutes.
3. Perform a coil fold (p. 35). Cover and let the dough rest for another 30 to 45 minutes.

Laminate the inclusions and proof (15 minutes active, 3–6 hours bulk proof at room temperature, overnight cold proof)

1. After the set time has elapsed, turn the dough out onto a clean, unfloured countertop and working from the middle, gently pull the dough out using your fingers to coax the dough to stretch further. Ensure slow stretching to prevent the dough from tearing. Moving around the edge of the dough, continue to pull it outward until you have achieved a roughly 15-inch (38cm) square.
2. Sprinkle half of the candied ginger and thyme over two-thirds of the dough. Take the corners of the third that does not have any inclusions and fold it like a letter until it is covering half of the inclusions. Fold it over again so you have a piece of dough that has been folded in thirds lengthwise. Sprinkle the remaining candied ginger and thyme over the length of dough and then roll it up from the bottom.
3. Place the dough back into the bowl, cover, and let it rest at room temperature until it is around doubled in size. This may take 3 to 6 hours, depending on the ambient room temperature.
4. Once the dough has doubled in size, gently turn the dough out from the bowl and place it seam-side up into a banneton or linen-lined bowl of your choice. Cover with a bowl cover or plastic wrap and place it into the refrigerator for an overnight cold proof.

Bake and store the loaf (35–45 minutes)

1. In the morning, preheat the oven to 425°F (220°C) with a covered bread cloche placed inside. Turn your dough out onto a piece of parchment paper or dough sling.
2. Score the dough as desired. Bake the dough in the covered bread cloche for 25 minutes, then uncover and bake for an additional 10 to 15 minutes. Knock the bottom of the loaf and if it sounds hollow and the internal temperature has reached 205°F to 210°F (96°C to 99°C), it is fully baked. If the loaf does not sound hollow, place it back in the oven for 10 minutes or until fully baked.
3. Let the bread cool on a wire rack for at least 1 hour before slicing.
4. Store at room temperature in a resealable bag for up to 3 days or freeze in an airtight container or freezer bag for up to 2 months.

Total time: 36 hours
Active prep time: 35–40 minutes
Baking time: 40–45 minutes
Makes: 1 loaf

SPECIAL EQUIPMENT

Stand mixer fitted with a dough hook (optional)
Dutch oven/bread cloche (I use a Fourneau Grande)
Banneton (optional)
Bread lame (optional)

INGREDIENTS

Dough

280g tap water
100g active 100%-hydration sourdough starter
9g sea salt
325g bread flour
75g whole wheat flour

Inclusions

70g fresh-squeezed orange juice
110g dried cranberries, roughly chopped
20g orange zest (3 to 4 navel oranges)
45g light brown sugar

Orange Cranberry Loaf

Level up your sourdough by baking this simple, wintry loaf that can be enjoyed with just a bit of butter and honey or made into a delectable French toast! The tender crumb is studded with fruit and zest, and the golden crust adds a perfect crunch. Bursting with the vibrant flavors of citrus and cranberry, this loaf is sure to be a hit during the holiday season.

Prepare the inclusions (5 minutes)

1. In a small bowl, combine the orange juice and dried cranberries. Set aside.
2. In a separate small bowl, combine the orange zest and brown sugar. Using your fingertips, rub them together. Set aside.

Prepare the dough (15 minutes active, 2 hours rest)

1. In a medium bowl or the bowl of a stand mixer, combine the water, starter, salt, bread flour, and whole wheat flour. Knead on low or mix by hand until the ingredients are incorporated. Cover the dough with a bowl cover or plastic wrap and let it rest for 30 to 45 minutes.
2. Perform a stretch-and-fold (p. 34). Cover and let the dough rest for another 30 to 45 minutes.
3. Perform a coil fold (p. 35). Cover and let the dough rest for another 30 to 45 minutes.

Laminate the inclusions and proof (15 minutes active, 3–6 hour bulk proof at room temperature, overnight cold proof)

1. After the set time has elapsed, turn the dough out onto a clean, unfloured countertop and, from the middle, gently pull the dough out using your fingers to coax the dough to stretch further. Ensure slow stretching to prevent the dough from tearing. Moving around the edge of the dough, continue to pull it outward until you have achieved a roughly 15-inch (38cm) square.
2. Drain any orange juice from the cranberry-and-juice mixture. Take half the sugar-zest mixture and using your fingers, rub it onto two-thirds of the dough. Take half of the cranberry mixture and sprinkle it evenly over the top of the sugar-zest mixture. Take the corners of the third that does not have any inclusions and fold it until it is covering half of the inclusions. Fold it over again so you have a piece of dough that has been folded in thirds lengthwise.
3. Rub the remaining sugar-zest mixture across the length of the dough and sprinkle the remaining cranberries on top of that. Roll it up from the bottom.
4. Place the dough back into the bowl, cover, and let it rest at room temperature until it has about doubled in size. This may take roughly 3 to 6 hours depending on the ambient room temperature.
5. Once the dough has doubled in size, gently turn the dough out from the bowl and place it seam-side up into a banneton or linen-lined bowl of your choice. You may notice some weeping from the dough. Wipe up any liquid with a paper towel or cotton cloth. Cover with a bowl cover or plastic wrap and place it in the refrigerator for an overnight cold proof.

Bake and store the loaf (40–45 minutes)

1. In the morning, preheat the oven to 425°F (220°C) with a covered bread cloche placed inside. Turn your dough out onto a piece of parchment paper or a dough sling.

2. Score the dough as desired. Bake the dough in the covered bread cloche for 35 minutes, then uncover and bake for an additional 5 to 10 minutes. Knock the bottom of the loaf and if it sounds hollow and the internal temperature has reached 195°F (91°C), it is fully baked. If the loaf does not sound hollow, place it back in the oven for 5-minute increments. (Keep an eye on this loaf, as the added sugar will cause the crust to brown very quickly!)
3. Let the bread cool on a rack for at least 1 hour before slicing.
4. Store at room temperature in a resealable bag for up to 3 days or freeze in an airtight container or freezer bag for up to 2 months.

Total time: 36 hours
Active prep time: 30 minutes
Baking time: 40 minutes
Makes: 1 loaf

EQUIPMENT

Stand mixer (optional)
Dutch oven/bread cloche (I use a Fourneau Grande)
Banneton (optional)
Bread lame (optional)

INGREDIENTS

Dough

280g tap water
100g active 100%-hydration sourdough starter
9g sea salt
325g bread flour
75g whole wheat flour

Inclusions

60g diced fresh jalapeño peppers, seeds removed
120g sharp cheddar, cut into ¼-inch (6mm) cubes

Jalapeño Cheddar Loaf

Level up your sourdough repertoire with this savory and slightly spicy loaf. Bursting with gooey pockets of sharp cheddar and the fresh heat of diced jalapeños, this bread is perfect for a hearty sandwich, alongside chili, or enjoyed simply toasted with butter. Its golden crust and tender crumb make it a crowd-pleasing favorite for any meal or occasion.

Prepare the dough (15 minutes plus 2–3 hours for gluten development)

1. In a medium bowl or the bowl of a stand mixer, combine the water, starter, honey, salt, bread flour, and whole wheat flour. Knead on low or mix by hand until the ingredients are incorporated. Cover the dough with a bowl cover or plastic wrap and let it rest for 30 to 45 minutes.
2. Perform a stretch-and-fold (p. 34). Cover and let the dough rest for another 30 to 45 minutes.
3. Perform a coil fold (p. 35). Cover and let the dough rest for another 30 to 45 minutes.

Laminate the inclusions (15 minutes plus 3–6 hours proofing)

1. After the set time has elapsed, turn the dough out onto a clean, unfloured countertop and from the middle, gently pull the dough out using your fingers to coax the dough to stretch further. Ensure slow stretching to prevent the dough from tearing. Moving around the edge of the dough, continue to pull it outward until you have achieved a roughly 15-inch (38cm) square.
2. Sprinkle half of the jalapeños and cheddar over two-thirds of the dough. Take the corners of the third that do not have any inclusions and fold it until it is covering half of the inclusions. Fold it over again, so you have a piece of dough that has been folded in thirds lengthwise. Sprinkle the remaining jalapeños and cheddar along the length of dough. Roll it up from the bottom.
3. Place the dough back into the bowl, cover it, and let it rest at room temperature until it has about doubled in size. This may take roughly 3 to 6 hours, depending on the ambient room temperature.
4. Once the dough has doubled in size, gently turn the dough out from the bowl and place it seam-side up into a banneton or linen-lined bowl of your choice. Cover the banneton with a bowl cover or plastic wrap and place it in the refrigerator for an overnight cold proof.

Bake and store the loaf (35 minutes)

1. In the morning, preheat the oven to 450°F (230°C) with a covered bread cloche placed inside. Turn your dough out onto a piece of parchment paper or a dough sling.
2. Score the dough as desired. Bake the dough in the covered bread cloche for 30 minutes, then uncover and bake for an additional 10 minutes. Knock the bottom of the loaf and if it sounds hollow and the internal temperature has reached 205°F to 210°F (96°C to 99°C), it is fully baked. If the loaf does not sound hollow, place it back in the oven for 10 minutes.
3. Let the bread cool on a rack for at least 1 hour before slicing.
4. Store at room temperature in a resealable bag for up to 3 days or freeze in an airtight container or freezer bag for up to 2 months.

Total time: 36 hours
Active prep time: 35 minutes
Baking time: 40–45 minutes
Makes: 1 loaf

EQUIPMENT

Stand mixer fitted with a dough hook (optional)
Dutch oven/bread cloche (I use a Fourneau Grande)
Banneton (optional)
Bread lame (optional)

INGREDIENTS

Dough
280g tap water
100g active 100%-hydration sourdough starter
9g sea salt
325g bread flour
75g whole wheat flour

Inclusions
50g granulated sugar
3g ground cinnamon
120g raisins

Cinnamon-Raisin Swirl Loaf

This Cinnamon-Raisin Swirl Loaf is as beautiful as it is delicious. Slicing through the crispy crust to the tender crumb reveals a mesmerizing spiral of cinnamon and raisins. The very subtle tang of sourdough elevates the flavors and aroma of this loaf. Enjoy with just a pat of butter, or make a rich French toast that is sure to be enjoyed by all!

Prepare the inclusions (3 minutes)

1. In a small bowl, mix the sugar and cinnamon. Set aside.

Prepare the dough (15 minutes plus 3–10 hours proofing)

1. In a medium bowl or the bowl of a stand mixer, combine the water, starter, salt, bread flour, and whole wheat flour. Knead on low or mix by hand until the ingredients are incorporated. Cover the dough with a bowl cover or plastic wrap and let it rest for 30 to 45 minutes.
2. Perform a stretch-and-fold (p. 34). Cover and let the dough rest for another 30 to 45 minutes.
3. Perform a coil fold (p. 35). Cover the dough and let it rest for another 30 to 45 minutes.

Laminate the inclusions and proof (15 minutes active, 3–6 hour bulk proof at room temperature, overnight cold proof)

1. After the set time has elapsed, turn the dough out onto a clean, unfloured countertop and, from the middle, gently pull the dough out using your fingers to coax the dough to stretch further. Ensure slow stretching to prevent the dough from tearing. Moving around the edge of the dough, continue to pull it outward until you have achieved a roughly 15-inch (38cm) square.
2. Sprinkle half of the cinnamon-sugar mixture and half of the raisins onto two-thirds of the dough. Take the corners of the third that do not have any inclusions and fold it until it is covering half of the inclusions. Fold it over again so you have a piece of dough that has been folded in thirds lengthwise. Sprinkle the remaining cinnamon-sugar mixture over the dough and then sprinkle the remaining raisins on top of that. Roll it up from the bottom.
3. Place the dough back into the bowl, cover, and let it rest at room temperature until it has around doubled in size. This may take 3 to 6 hours depending on the ambient room temperature.
4. Once the dough has doubled in size, gently turn the dough out from the bowl and place it seam-side up into a banneton or linen-lined bowl of your choice. Cover with a bowl cover or plastic wrap and place it into the refrigerator for an overnight cold proof.

Bake and store the loaf (40–45 minutes)

1. In the morning, preheat the oven to 425°F (220°C) with a covered bread cloche placed inside.
2. Turn the dough out onto a piece of parchment paper or a dough sling.
3. Score the dough as desired. Bake the dough in the covered bread cloche for 35 minutes, then uncover and bake for an additional 5 to 10 minutes. (Keep an

eye on this loaf, as the added sugar will cause the crust to brown very quickly!) Knock the bottom of the loaf. If it sounds hollow, and the internal temperature has reached 205°F to 210°F (96°C to 99°C), it is fully baked. If the loaf does not sound hollow, place it back in the oven for 10 minutes.

4. Let the bread cool on a rack for at least 1 hour before slicing.
5. Store at room temperature in a resealable bag for up to 3 days or freeze in an airtight container or freezer bag for up to 2 months.

CHAPTER 5

Enriched Loaves

Soft White Sandwich Bread

Total time: 36 hours
Active prep time: 40 minutes
Baking time: 40–50 minutes
Makes: 1 loaf

SPECIAL EQUIPMENT

Stand mixer fitted with a dough hook (optional)
One 8.5 × 4.75 × 4.375-inch (22 × 12 × 11cm) Pullman loaf pan

INGREDIENTS

230g tap water
250g 100%-hydration active sourdough starter
50g honey
10g sea salt
500g white bread flour
80g unsalted butter, softened and divided
1 medium egg (for egg wash), optional

Skip the bread aisle at the grocery store! Your kiddos are going to want no other sandwich bread than this one. Made with a generous amount of sourdough starter, this bread is the perfect balance between flavor and texture, and it can be enjoyed by everyone. With the addition of honey and butter, this enriched bread is going to become a regular in your sourdough baking regime.

Make and proof the dough (30–40 minutes, 4–10 hour bulk proof at room temperature, overnight cold proof)

1. In a medium bowl or the bowl of a stand mixer, combine the water, starter, honey, salt, and flour. Knead on low or mix by hand until fully combined, about 5 minutes.
2. Add half the butter and knead until fully combined. Add the remaining butter and knead for 20 minutes. (You may also knead the dough by hand for around 30 minutes.)
3. Place the dough in a medium bowl, if not already in one, and cover with a bowl cover or plastic wrap. Proof at room temperature until it has doubled in volume. (This may take 4 to 10 hours depending on the ambient room temperature.) Place the covered bowl in the refrigerator for an overnight cold proof.

Shape and proof the dough (10 minutes active, 4–8 hour proof at room temperature)

1. The next morning, prepare the loaf pan by coating it with butter or cooking spray.
2. Remove the dough from refrigerator, and lightly flour a work surface. Using a rolling pin, roll the dough out to an 8 × 16-inch (20 × 41cm) rectangle.
3. Roll the dough into a log starting at the short side and place it seam-side down in the prepared loaf pan.
4. Cover with a bowl cover or plastic wrap and allow the dough to proof at room temperature until puffy and a finger-poke test produces a slow return of the dough. (This may take 4 to 8 hours depending on the ambient room temperature.)

Bake and store the loaf (40–50 minutes)

1. Preheat the oven to 375°F (190°C).
2. Whisk the egg (if using) in a small bowl. Use a pastry brush to coat the dough in the egg wash.
3. Bake, uncovered, for 40 to 50 minutes or until the internal temperature reaches 195°F (91°C). Let the bread cool on a wire rack for 1 hour before slicing.
4. Store at room temperature in a resealable bag for up to 3 days or freeze in an airtight container or freezer bag for up to 2 months.

Total time: 8–30 hours
Active prep time: 25 minutes
Baking time: 50–60 minutes
Makes: 1 loaf

SPECIAL EQUIPMENT

Stand mixer fitted with a dough hook (optional)
One 8.5 x 4.75 x 4.375-inch (22 × 12 × 11cm) Pullman loaf pan

INGREDIENTS

265g tap water
225g 100%-hydration active sourdough starter
80g honey
10g sea salt
250g white bread flour
250g whole wheat flour
50g unsalted butter, softened and divided

Honey Whole Wheat Sandwich Bread

This soft, fluffy sandwich bread will be a treat for the whole family! It can be made the same day as long as the ambient room temperature is warm enough. In cooler months, however, it may better suit your schedule to spread the process out over two days. Enjoy it with a pat of butter or deck it into a full sandwich; either way, you're going to love this whole wheat sandwich loaf!

Make and proof the dough (20 minutes active, 4–10 hours bulk proof at room temperature, optional overnight cold proof)

1. In a medium bowl or the bowl of a stand mixer, combine the water, starter, honey, salt, bread flour, and whole wheat flour. Knead on low or mix by hand until fully combined, about 5 minutes. Add half the butter and knead until fully combined. Add the remaining butter and knead for 20 minutes. (You may also knead the dough by hand for around 30 minutes.)
2. Place the dough in a medium bowl, if not already in one, and cover with a bowl cover or plastic wrap. Proof at room temperature until it has doubled in volume. (This may take 4 to 10 hours depending on the ambient room temperature.)
3. If you wish to bake the loaf on the same day, proceed directly to the next section. Otherwise, place the covered bowl in the refrigerator for an overnight cold proof.

Shape and proof the dough (5 minutes active, 2–6 hours room-temperature proof)

1. The next morning, prepare the loaf pan by coating it with butter or cooking spray.
2. Remove the dough from the refrigerator, and lightly flour a work surface. Using a rolling pin, roll the dough out to an 8 × 16-inch (20 × 41cm) rectangle.
3. Roll the dough into a log starting at the short side and then place it seam-side down in the prepared loaf pan.
4. Cover with a bowl cover or plastic wrap and allow the dough to proof at room temperature until puffy, and a finger-poke test produces a slow return of the dough. (This may take 2 to 6 hours depending on the ambient room temperature.) Note that if you decide to make it on the same day, it will proof much faster.

Bake and store the loaf (50–60 minutes)

1. Preheat the oven to 370°F (188°C).
2. Bake the dough for 50 to 60 minutes or until the internal temperature reaches 205°F (96°C). Let the bread cool on a wire rack for 1 hour before slicing.
3. Store at room temperature in a resealable bag for up to 3 days or freeze in an airtight container or freezer bag for up to 2 months.

Fluffy Challah Bread

Total time: 40 hours
Active prep time:
1 hour 15 minutes
Baking time: 35–45 minutes
Makes: 2 challah loaves

SPECIAL EQUIPMENT

Stand mixer fitted with a dough hook (optional)

INGREDIENTS

Sweet stiff starter

50g 100%-hydration unfed sourdough starter
66g tap water
120g all-purpose flour
20g granulated sugar

Dough

95g tap water
All of the sweet stiff starter
9g sea salt
80g granulated sugar
5 medium eggs, divided
560g white bread flour
50g neutral oil (I use avocado oil)

Coating

Up to 120g sesame seeds (optional)

This naturally leavened challah bread is light, fluffy, and perfect for any occasion. Using a sweet stiff sourdough starter adds a gentle sweetness, yielding a bread that is soft and airy, without a sour edge. Enjoy it fresh out of the oven!

Prepare the starter (5 minutes active, 12 hours rise)

1. Prepare the sweet stiff starter the night before making the dough by mixing all starter ingredients together in a 1-liter (34fl oz) container. Cover the starter with plastic wrap and let it rise until at peak or has just started to fall (at least 12 hours).

Make and proof the dough (30–40 minutes active, 3–10 hours bulk proof at room temperature, overnight cold proof)

1. The next morning, to a medium bowl or the bowl of a stand mixer, add the water, starter, salt, sugar, 4 eggs, and flour. Mix on low for 10 minutes or knead by hand for 15 minutes or until the ingredients are fully incorporated.
2. Gradually add the oil to the dough in small amounts, kneading by hand for 30 minutes or in the stand mixer for about 20 minutes until smooth and elastic. (Note: You can proof the dough in the stand mixer bowl, however, I typically transfer the dough to a medium bowl to proof. Also, this is a very high-hydration dough. Don't fret! Higher hydration makes it much easier to roll out the strands for braiding. If you do find it to be too difficult to handle, you may add an additional 10 to 30 grams of flour.)
3. *(Optional gluten development for a more shreddable crumb. If you wish to skip this step, proceed to step 4.)* Once 30 minutes have elapsed, perform a coil fold (p. 35). Perform two more coil folds in 30-minute intervals.
4. Cover the dough with a bowl cover or plastic wrap and let the dough proof until it has doubled in volume. (This may take 3 to 10 hours depending on the ambient room temperature.) Place the covered dough in the refrigerator for an overnight cold proof.

Shape and proof the dough (20–30 minutes active, 30 minutes rest, 2–8 hours proof)

1. The next morning, line two large cookie sheets with parchment paper.
2. Remove the dough from the refrigerator. Divide it into six equal-size portions and then roll the portions into 8-inch (20cm) logs. Cover the logs with a tea towel and let them rest for 30 minutes.
3. Roll the logs to 16 inches (41cm). If you want to coat some or part of the loaf in sesame seeds, fill a shallow bowl with water. Pour the sesame seeds into a separate bowl. Dip a log in the water and immediately place it in the bowl of sesame seeds. Rotate the log in the seeds until fully coated. Repeat with the remaining logs, if desired. Braid into two 3-strand loaves. Place each loaf on a parchment-lined cookie sheet.
4. Cover the loaves with plastic wrap and allow them to double in size or until they're puffy and a finger-poke test produces a slow return of the dough. (This may take 2 to 8 hours depending on the ambient room temperature.)

Bake and store the challah (35–45 minutes)

1. Preheat the oven to 365°F (185°C). Whisk the remaining egg in a small bowl to create the egg wash. Brush the tops of the uncoated parts of the loaves with the egg wash.
2. Bake for 35 to 45 minutes until golden or the internal temperature reaches 195°F (91°C). Enjoy warm.
3. Store at room temperature in a resealable bag for up to 3 days or freeze in an airtight container or freezer bag for up to 2 months.

Total time: 42 hours
Active prep time:
1 hour 15 minutes
Baking time:
50–60 minutes
Makes: 1 loaf

SPECIAL EQUIPMENT

Stand mixer fitted with a dough hook (optional)
One 8.5 × 4.75 × 4.375-inch (22 × 12 × 11cm) Pullman loaf pan

INGREDIENTS

Sweet stiff starter

50g unfed 100%-hydration sourdough starter
66g tap water
20g granulated sugar
120g all-purpose flour

Dough

50g any type of milk (I use 2%)
All the sweet stiff starter
8g sea salt
80g granulated sugar
5 medium eggs, divided
400g bread flour
113g unsalted butter, softened and divided

Buttery Brioche

This light, airy brioche features a beautifully shreddable texture and presents near-endless possibilities. Whether you transform it into a soft French toast, shape it into burger buns, or enjoy it fresh from the oven, the result is sure to please! Because the dough relies on a higher fat content and a sweet stiff starter, it does take a bit more time to proof, but trust me—the wait is absolutely worth it. Enjoy the irresistible aroma, taste, and versatility of this classic brioche in all its forms.

Prepare the sweet stiff starter (5 minutes, 12 hours rise)

1. Prepare the sweet stiff starter the night before making the dough by mixing all starter ingredients together in a 1-liter (34fl oz) container. Cover the starter with plastic wrap and let it rise until at peak or has just started to fall, at least 12 hours.

Make and proof the dough (40 minutes active, 4–10 hours bulk proof at room temperature, overnight cold proof)

1. The next morning, in a medium bowl or the bowl of a stand mixer, add the milk, sweet stiff starter, salt, sugar, 4 eggs, and flour. Mix on low for 10 minutes. Alternatively, knead by hand for 15 minutes or until the ingredients are fully incorporated.
2. Gradually add the butter to the dough, 1 to 2 tablespoons at a time, kneading until the butter is fully incorporated after each addition. Knead by hand or in the stand mixer for 20 to 30 minutes until the dough is smooth and elastic. Cover the dough with a bowl cover or plastic wrap and let it rest for 1 hour.
3. *(Optional gluten development for a more shreddable crumb. If you wish to skip this step, proceed to step 4.)* Once 1 hour has elapsed, perform a coil fold (p. 35). Perform two more coil folds in 30-minute intervals.
4. Cover the dough with a bowl cover or plastic wrap and let the dough proof until it has doubled in volume. This may take 4 to 10 hours depending on the ambient room temperature. (Note that the high quantity of sugar and butter in this recipe can often slow fermentation.) Place the covered dough in the refrigerator for an overnight cold proof.

Shape and proof (30 minutes active, 20 minutes rest, plus 3–8 hours for final proof)

1. The next morning, remove the cold dough from the refrigerator. Remove the dough from the bowl and on a lightly floured work surface, roughly form it into a log. Using a bench scraper, divide the log into four equal-size portions from the short side. The pieces should look like rectangles. Let the rectangles rest, covered with a kitchen towel, for 20 minutes.
2. While the dough is resting, prepare your loaf pan by spraying it with nonstick cooking spray or rubbing the pan with butter.
3. Once 20 minutes have elapsed, use a rolling pin to roll the rectangles into 5 × 8-inch (13 × 20cm) pieces. Fold the sides into the middle to create 2.5 x 8-inch (6 x 20cm) rectangles.
4. With a rolling pin, roll these pieces out to 3.5 × 11-inch (9 × 28cm). From the bottom of the short side, roll up the dough loosely to create a cylinder. Place the cylinder in the prepared loaf pan, seam-side down. Repeat this process with the other three portions of dough and place them in the loaf pan.

5. Cover the dough with a bowl cover or plastic wrap and proof until the dough has doubled in size, looks airy and puffy, and a finger-poke test produces a slow return of the dough. (This may take 3 to 8 hours depending on the ambient room temperature.)

Bake and store the loaf (50–60 minutes)

1. Preheat the oven to 350°F (175°C). Whisk the remaining egg in a small bowl and brush the top of the loaf using a pastry brush for a glossy finish.
2. Bake, uncovered, for 50 to 60 minutes or until the loaf is golden brown and the internal temperature reaches 200°F (93°C).
3. Let the dough rest in the pan for 5 minutes on the wire rack. Then remove the loaf and let cool for 1 hour on a wire rack before slicing.
4. Store at room temperature in a resealable bag for up to 3 days or freeze in an airtight container or freezer bag for up to 2 months.

Total time: 36 hours
Active prep time: 40 minutes
Baking time: 40–50 minutes
Makes: 1 loaf

SPECIAL EQUIPMENT

Stand mixer fitted with a dough hook (optional)
One 8.5 × 4.75 × 4.375-inch (22 × 12 × 11cm) Pullman loaf pan

---

INGREDIENTS

Dough

210g tap water
235g 100%-hydration active sourdough starter
55g honey
10g sea salt
475g white bread flour
65g unsalted butter, softened and divided
80g raisins (soaked for 10 minutes and then drained)
1 medium egg (for egg wash), optional

Cinnamon swirl

30g granulated sugar
4g ground cinnamon

Enriched Cinnamon-Raisin Swirl Loaf

This fluffy, enriched bread is a classic with a sourdough twist. It is soft and buttery with a warm cinnamon swirl and juicy raisins throughout. Enjoy a slice toasted with a slab of butter for breakfast, or zhuzh it up by making some French toast and serving it for brunch!

Make and proof the dough (30–40 minutes active, 4–10 hour bulk proof at room temperature, overnight cold proof)

1. In a medium bowl or the bowl of a stand mixer, combine the water, starter, honey, salt, and flour. Knead on low or mix by hand until fully combined, about 5 minutes. Add half the butter and knead until fully combined. Add the remaining butter and knead for 20 minutes. (You may also knead the dough by hand for around 30 minutes.)
2. Add the raisins and knead on low just until incorporated (or fold them in by hand).
3. Place the dough in a medium bowl, if not already in one, and cover with a bowl cover or plastic wrap. Proof at room temperature until the dough has doubled in volume. (This may take 4 to 10 hours depending on the ambient room temperature.) Place the covered bowl in the refrigerator for an overnight cold proof.

Shape and proof the dough (10 minutes active, 4–8 hour room-temperature proof)

1. The next morning, prepare the loaf pan by coating it with butter or cooking spray.
2. Remove the dough from the refrigerator. Sprinkle the work surface lightly with flour and, using a rolling pin, roll it out to an 8 × 16-inch (20 × 41cm) rectangle.
3. In a small bowl, mix the sugar and cinnamon. Sprinkle the mixture evenly over the dough, leaving a ½-inch (1.25cm) border.
4. Roll the dough into a log starting at the short side and then place it seam-side down in the prepared loaf pan.
5. Cover with a bowl cover or plastic wrap and allow the dough to proof at room temperature until puffy and a finger-poke test produces a slow return of the dough. (This may take 4 to 8 hours depending on the ambient room temperature.)

Bake and store the loaf (40–50 minutes)

1. Preheat the oven to 375°F (190°C).
2. Whisk the egg (if using) in a small bowl. Use a pastry brush to coat the dough in the egg wash.
3. Bake for 40 to 50 minutes or until the internal temperature reaches 195°F (91°C). Let the bread cool on a wire rack for 1 hour before slicing.
4. Store at room temperature in a resealable bag for up to 3 days or freeze in an airtight container or freezer bag for up to 2 months.

CHAPTER 6

Rolls and Buns

Total time: 36 hours
Active prep time: 40 minutes
Baking time: 18–20 minutes
Makes: 4 demi-baguettes

SPECIAL EQUIPMENT
Dough whisk (optional)
Bench scraper
Bread cloche or baking steel or stone (I use a Fourneau Grande)
Stiff linen bread couche or linen cloth
Bread lame

INGREDIENTS
400g tap water
160g 100%-hydration sourdough starter
12g fine sea salt
600g Tipo 65 flour or all-purpose flour

Demi-Baguettes

My demi-baguette recipe is one of my all-time favorites. It's the perfect loaf for wrapping around all your favorite fillings. (I'm partial to banh mi.) While the shaping can be a bit of a challenge, the payoff is more than worth it—a crispy, blistered crust and a lacy crumb that's deeply satisfying to bite into and absolutely delicious.

Mix and proof the dough (30 minutes active, 2–6 hours bulk proof at room temperature, overnight cold proof)

1. In a medium mixing bowl, combine all the dough ingredients and mix with a dough whisk, a wooden spoon, or your hands until well combined. Cover with a bowl cover or plastic wrap and let the dough rest for 45 minutes.
2. After the allotted time has elapsed, perform a stretch-and-fold (p. 34). Cover and rest for 45 minutes more.
3. Over the next 3 to 4 hours, perform 4 sets of coil folds (p. 35) spaced 30 to 45 minutes apart. Cover and let the dough bulk proof at room temperature until the dough has increased in volume by about 50 to 60 percent. (This may take 2 to 6 hours depending on the ambient room temperature.) Place the covered bowl in the refrigerator for an overnight cold proof.

Preshape the dough (10 minutes active, 45 minutes rest)

1. In the morning, remove the dough from the fridge. Lightly sprinkle your work surface with all-purpose flour and turn the dough out onto the surface. Using a bench scraper, divide the dough into 4 equal-size pieces.
2. With floured fingers, gently degas the dough pieces and shape them into loose rectangles that measure roughly 2.5 × 4 inches (6 × 10cm) each.
3. Cover the dough pieces with a cotton tea towel and let them rest for 45 minutes.

Shape and proof the dough (10 minutes active, 2–5 hours room-temperature proof)

1. Flip each dough piece topside-down onto a lightly floured work surface. Gently pat the pieces out into 4 × 6-inch (10 × 15cm) rectangles. Fold the tops (long sides) into the middle of the dough. Rotate the pieces 180 degrees and fold them in half, bringing the edges together. Seal the edges with the heel of your hand, creating little cylinders. (See inset photos.)
2. Using your hands, gently roll out the cylinders to 10 inches (25cm), pressing more firmly toward the end of the cylinder to create a tapered shape. Place each baguette topside down in a linen baking couche or linen cloth dusted liberally with rice flour, lifting up the couche to create a barrier between each demi-baguette.
3. Allow the demi-baguettes to proof until doubled in size and a finger-poke test reveals a slow return of the dough. (This can take 2 to 5 hours depending on the ambient room temperature.)

Bake and store the demi-baguettes (18–20 minutes)

1. Preheat the oven to 500°F (260°C) with your bread cloche, baking steel, or stone in the oven. If you plan to do an "open bake" (not in a bread cloche, but on a stone or steel directly in the oven), place a deep, oven-safe tray in the bottom of the oven and bring a kettle of water to boil over high heat.
2. Flip the demi-baguettes onto a cutting board dusted with rice flour and slide them off onto parchment paper or a board to transfer the dough to the cloche or baking steel or stone.

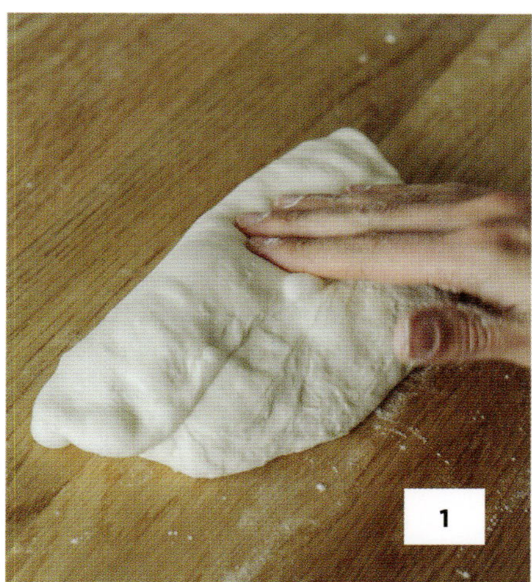

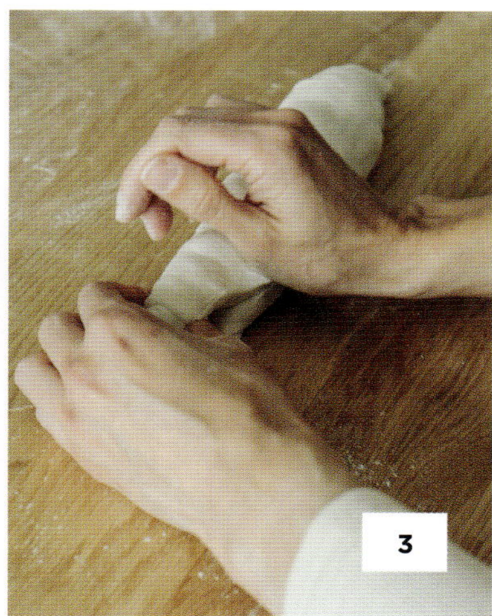

3. Use a bread lame to score 2 to 3 slightly slanted lines into the baguette dough and transfer the dough directly into the bread cloche or onto the bread steel or stone. Add ice to your cloche (to create steam) and cover. If you are doing an "open bake," very carefully fill the deep tray at the bottom with the boiling water. (Be very careful when adding the water, you can easily burn your skin while following this step.)
4. Bake for 15 minutes covered and then 6 minutes uncovered. If you did an "open bake," carefully remove the deep tray of water if it has not all evaporated. Bake until the crust is a deep golden brown or until the internal temperature measures 195°F (91°C).
5. Store the bread at room temperature in a resealable bag for up to 3 days or freeze in an airtight container or freezer bag for up to 2 months.

Total time: 42 hours
Active prep time: 1 hour 25 minutes
Baking time: 20–25 minutes
Makes: 15 dinner rolls

SPECIAL EQUIPMENT

Stand mixer fitted with a dough hook (optional)
One 9 × 13 × 2-inch (23 × 33 × 5cm) baking sheet

INGREDIENTS

Tangzhong

40g all-purpose flour
200g any type of milk (I use 2%)

Dough

100g any type of milk (I use 2%)
230g 100%-hydration active sourdough starter
40g granulated sugar
3 medium eggs, divided
All of the tangzhong
12g sea salt
600g bread flour
50g unsalted butter, softened

Soft Dinner Rolls

These pillowy sourdough dinner rolls are enjoyed best when they're still warm. Made with *tangzhong*, a paste created by cooking flour, water and/or milk, these rolls stay incredibly tender for days without any additives. The tangzhong allows the dough to absorb more water and hold onto moisture when baking, resulting in rolls that are fluffy and light. Combined with the addition of sourdough, these rolls have a beautiful depth of flavor with a subtle tang.

Make the tangzhong (5–10 minutes active, 15–20 minutes cooldown)

1. In a small heavy-bottomed pot, combine the milk and flour.
2. Whisk continuously over medium heat until the mixture reaches a consistency similar to mashed potatoes. Remove from the heat and allow to cool to room temperature.

Make and proof the dough (45 minutes active, 4–10 hours bulk proof at room temperature, overnight cold proof)

1. In a large bowl or the bowl of a stand mixer, combine the milk, starter, sugar, 2 eggs, tangzhong, salt, and flour. Knead on low or mix by hand until fully combined. Add half the butter and knead on low until fully combined. Add the remaining butter and knead on low for 20 minutes. (You may also knead the dough by hand for around 30 minutes.) Cover the dough with a bowl cover or plastic wrap and let it rest for 1 hour.
2. *(Optional step for gluten development for a more shreddable crumb. If you wish to skip this step, proceed to step 4.)* Once 1 hour has elapsed, perform a coil fold (p. 35). Perform two more coil folds in 30-minute intervals.
3. Cover the dough with a bowl cover or plastic wrap and let the dough proof until it has doubled in volume. (This may take 4 to 10 hours depending on the ambient room temperature.) Place the covered dough in the refrigerator for an overnight cold proof.

Shape and final proof (30 minutes active, 3–8 hours final proof)

4. The next morning, prepare a 9 × 13-inch (23 × 33cm) baking sheet by spraying it lightly with baking spray.
5. Turn the dough out onto a lightly floured surface. Use a bench scraper to divide it into 15 equal-size pieces.
6. Shape the pieces into smooth balls and arrange them, evenly spaced, in the prepared baking sheet.
7. Cover the rolls with plastic wrap and let them proof until they double in size, appear airy and puffy, and a finger-poke test produces a slow return of the dough. (This may take 3 to 8 hours depending on ambient room temperature.)

Bake and store the rolls (20–25 minutes)

1. Preheat the oven to 350°F (175°C). Whisk the remaining egg in a small bowl and brush the tops of the rolls using a pastry brush for a glossy finish.
2. Bake for 20 to 25 minutes or until the rolls are golden brown and the internal temperature reaches 195°F (91°C).
3. Let the rolls rest in the pan for 5 minutes on the wire rack, then remove the rolls from the pan and place them on the rack to allow them to cool further.
4. Store at room temperature in a resealable bag for up to 5 days or freeze in an airtight container or freezer bag for up to 2 months.

Total time: 36 hours
Active prep time:
55 minutes
Baking time: 15–20 minutes
Makes: 8 buns

SPECIAL EQUIPMENT

Stand mixer fitted with a dough hook (optional)

INGREDIENTS

Tangzhong

20g all-purpose flour
100g any type of milk (I use 2%)

Dough

80g any type of milk (I use 2%)
180g 100%-hydration active sourdough starter
55g honey
3 medium eggs, divided
1 medium egg yolk
All of the tangzhong
10g fine sea salt
450g all-purpose flour
80g unsalted butter, softened and divided

Soft Burger Buns

Why settle for store-bought when you can make the softest, fluffiest burger buns right at home? Made with *tangzhong*, a paste created by cooking flour, water and/or milk, these rolls stay incredibly tender for days without any additives. They're cloud-soft but sturdy enough to hold up to even the juiciest burgers. Once you taste them, you'll wonder why you ever bought burger buns from the store.

Make the tangzhong (5–10 minutes active, 15–20 minutes cooldown)

1. In a small heavy-bottomed pot, combine the flour and milk for the tangzhong.
2. Whisk continuously over medium heat until the mixture reaches a consistency similar to mashed potatoes. Remove from the heat and allow to cool to room temperature.

Make and proof the dough (25–30 minutes active, 4–10 hours bulk proof at room temperature, overnight cold proof)

1. In a medium bowl or the bowl of a stand mixer, combine the milk, starter, honey, 2 eggs, egg yolk, tangzhong, salt, and flour. Knead on low or mix by hand until fully combined. Add half the butter and knead on low until fully combined. Add the remaining butter and knead on low for 20 minutes. (You may also knead the dough by hand for around 30 minutes.)
2. Place the dough in a medium bowl, if not already in one, and cover with a bowl cover or plastic wrap. Proof at room temperature until it has doubled in volume. (This may take 4 to 10 hours depending on the ambient room temperature.) Place the covered dough in the refrigerator for an overnight cold proof.

Shape and final proof (10 minutes active, 3–8 hours final proof)

1. The next morning, prepare a baking sheet by lining it with parchment paper.
2. Turn the dough out onto a lightly floured surface, divide it into 8 equal-size pieces, then shape the pieces into balls. Using a rolling pin or the palm of your hand, flatten the balls until they are 3.5 inches (9cm) in diameter. Place the balls on the parchment-lined baking sheet.
3. Cover the dough loosely with plastic wrap and allow to proof at room temperature until puffy and doubled in size. (This may take 3 to 8 hours depending on the ambient room temperature.)

Bake and store the buns (15–20 minutes)

1. Preheat the oven to 375°F (190°C).
2. Whisk the remaining egg in a small bowl. Brush the buns with the egg wash. Bake the buns for 15 to 20 minutes or until the internal temperature reaches 195°F (91°C). Let the buns cool on a wire rack for 30 minutes before slicing.
3. Store the buns at room temperature in an airtight container or resealable bag for up to 5 days or freeze in a freezer bag for up to 2 months.

Total time: 36 hours
Active prep time: 40–50 minutes
Baking time: 20–25 minutes
Makes: 15 garlic knots

SPECIAL EQUIPMENT

Stand mixer fitted with a dough hook (optional)
Bench scraper
One 9 × 13 × 2-inch (23 × 33 × 5cm) baking sheet

INGREDIENTS

Tangzhong

100g any type of milk (I use 2%)
100g tap water
40g all-purpose flour

Dough

100g any type of milk (I use 2%)
230g 100%-hydration active sourdough starter
40g granulated sugar
All of the tangzhong
2 medium eggs
12g sea salt
600g bread flour
50g unsalted butter, softened to room temperature

Garlic spread

100g unsalted butter, melted
4 cloves garlic, finely grated or minced
1 tbsp finely chopped fresh parsley
2g fine sea salt
10g Parmesan cheese, grated

Garlic Knots

Perfectly pillowy and emboldened with the flavor of garlic and parsley, these garlic knots are the ultimate crowd pleaser! Whether served alongside a warm bowl of pasta or as a solo snack, they are completely irresistible.

Prepare the tangzhong (5–10 minutes active, 15–20 minutes cooldown)

1. In a small heavy-bottomed pot, combine the milk, water, and flour. Whisk continuously over medium heat until the mixture reaches a thick, pudding-like consistency. Remove from the heat and allow to cool to room temperature.

Make and proof the dough (45 minutes active, 3–10 hour bulk proof at room temperature, overnight cold proof)

1. In a large bowl or the bowl of a stand mixer, combine the milk, starter, sugar, tangzhong, eggs, salt, and flour. Knead on low or mix by hand until fully combined, about 5 minutes. Add half the butter and knead on low until fully combined. Add the remaining butter and knead on low for 20 minutes. (You may knead the dough by hand for around 30 minutes instead.) Cover the dough with a bowl cover or plastic wrap and let it rest for 30 minutes.
2. *(Optional gluten development for a more shreddable crumb. If you wish to skip this step, proceed to step 3.)* Once 30 minutes have elapsed, perform a coil fold (p. 35). Perform two more coil folds in 30-minute intervals, covering the dough in between folds.
3. Let the dough proof until it has doubled in volume. (This may take 3 to 10 hours depending on the ambient room temperature.) Place the covered dough in the refrigerator for an overnight cold proof.

Shape and final proof (30 minutes active, 3–8 hour final proof)

1. The next morning, prepare the baking sheet by lining it with parchment paper.
2. Turn the dough out onto a lightly floured surface and, using a bench scraper, divide it into 15 equal-size pieces.
3. Roll each piece of dough into a rope about 8 to 10 inches (20 to 25cm) long. (Try to maintain an even thickness.) Gently tie the rope into a simple knot by crossing the right end over the left to form an X. Take the end that is on top (the right end) and bring it underneath the other end and through the hole that has been made. Pull both ends gently to tighten the loop lightly. Place each knot onto the baking sheet and then cover with plastic wrap. Let the knots proof until they appear airy and puffy and a finger-poke test produces a slow return of the dough. (This may take 3 to 8 hours depending on the ambient room temperature.)

Bake the rolls, prepare the spread, and store (20–25 minutes)

1. Preheat the oven to 375°F (190°C).
2. Bake the knots for 20 to 25 minutes or until golden brown and the internal temperature reaches 195°F (91°C).
3. Let the knots rest in the pan for 5 minutes, then transfer to a wire rack.
4. While the knots are cooling, prepare the garlic spread by mixing together all ingredients in a small bowl. Brush or spoon the spread onto the still-warm knots. Serve immediately. If you are planning to store the knots, do not brush them with the garlic spread until they are ready to be eaten.
5. Store the uncoated knots at room temperature in a resealable bag for up to 5 days or freeze for up to 2 months in an airtight container or freezer bag.

Total time: 32–48 hours
Active prep time: 1 hour
Baking time: 20–25 minutes
Makes: 8 ciabatta rolls

SPECIAL EQUIPMENT

Bench scraper
Stiff linen bread couche or linen cloth

INGREDIENTS

450g tap water
200g 100%-hydration active sourdough starter
25g extra-virgin olive oil
12g sea salt
600g bread flour
Rice flour (for dusting)

Ciabatta

These delightful, rustic rolls made with a sourdough twist are the perfect sandwich bread. The shaping of these rolls is so straightforward; this will be a go-to recipe for the rest of your sourdough-making years! Enjoy them as a sandwich or fresh out of the oven with just a slab of butter.

Mix and proof the dough (30 minutes active, 4–8 hours bulk proof at room temperature, overnight cold proof)

1. In a medium mixing bowl, combine all the dough ingredients and mix with a dough whisk, a wooden spoon, or your hands until well combined. Cover with a bowl cover or plastic wrap and let the dough rest for 30 to 45 minutes.
2. After the allotted time has elapsed, perform a stretch-and-fold (p. 34). Cover and let rest for 45 minutes more.
3. Over the next 3 to 4 hours, perform four sets of coil folds spaced 30 to 45 minutes apart. Cover and let the dough bulk proof at room temperature until nearly doubled in size. (This may take 4 to 8 hours depending on the ambient room temperature.) Place the covered bowl in the refrigerator for an overnight cold proof.

Shape the dough and final proof (5 minutes active, 4–8 hours final proof)

1. The next morning, prepare the bread couche or linen cloth by dusting it liberally with rice flour.
2. Remove the dough from the fridge and turn it out onto a well-floured counter. Gently shape it into a 8 x 16-inch (20 x 41cm) rectangle.
3. Use a bench scraper to cut the dough into eight equal-size rectangles. Dust the tops with rice flour and gently turn them onto the bread couche. Lift a portion of the couche to create a barrier between the buns. Cover the rolls with a linen tea towel and let them proof until they appear airy and have doubled in size.

Bake and store the ciabatta (20–25 minutes)

1. Preheat the oven to 450°F (230°C). Bring a kettle of water to a boil over high heat.
2. Prepare a baking sheet by lining it with parchment paper.
3. Place a deep, oven-safe tray in the bottom of the oven.
4. Using the bench scraper, gently lift each roll and transfer it to the parchment paper–lined baking sheet.
5. Place the ciabatta in the oven on the middle rack. Very carefully fill the deep tray at the bottom of the oven halfway with the boiling water. (Be very careful when adding the water, you can easily burn your skin while following this step.)
6. Bake the ciabatta for 20 to 25 minutes or until the internal temperature measures 195°F (91°C).
7. Transfer the rolls to a wire rack and allow them to cool for 30 minutes before slicing.
8. Store the bread at room temperature in a resealable bag for up to 3 days or freeze in an airtight container or freezer bag for up to 2 months.

Total time: 36 hours
Active prep time: 30 minutes
Baking time: 20–25 minutes
Makes: 4 buns

SPECIAL EQUIPMENT
Dough whisk (optional)

INGREDIENTS
350g tap water
400g white bread flour
100g 100%-hydration active sourdough starter
8g sea salt

Pan de Cristal

Also known as "glass bread," this bread originates from Spain and is beloved for its delicate crust and airy crumb. It's the perfect bread to use for sandwiches or just on its own dipped in olive oil. This dough is very wet and slack, and developing its structure takes time and care. Coil folds are essential but not easy; be gentle and avoid overstretching the dough or it will tear. I like to lift just above the rim of the bowl and keep the folds short and quick. High-protein flour is a non-negotiable for this recipe; you need the protein content to be over 12 percent or the dough simply will not come together.

Make and proof the dough (30 minutes active, 3–6 hours room-temperature bulk ferment, overnight cold proof)

1. In a medium bowl, using your hands or a dough whisk, mix the water and flour until fully combined. Cover with a bowl cover or plastic wrap and let the dough rest for 1 hour.
2. Add the starter and salt to the bowl and mix until fully incorporated. Cover and let the dough rest for 30 minutes.
3. Perform one stretch-and-fold (p. 34). Cover and rest for another 30 minutes.
4. Over the next 3 hours, perform four or five coil folds (p. 35), resting the dough for 30 minutes between each fold. It's important to ensure the dough does not tear during the coil folds. Work quickly and gently to avoid overstretching the dough.
5. After the final fold, cover and let the dough rest at room temperature until it has doubled in size. (This may take 3 to 6 hours depending on the ambient room temperature.) Place the covered dough in the refrigerator for an overnight cold proof.

Shape and final proof (20 minutes active, 2–5 hours final proof)

1. The next morning, prepare a baking sheet by lining it with parchment paper.
2. Gently turn the dough out onto a well-floured surface, shape it into a 12-inch (30cm) square, and dust the top of the dough generously with flour. Then use a bench scraper to divide it into four equal-size pieces.
3. Carefully transfer each piece to the baking sheet, spacing them 2 to 3 inches (5 to 8cm) apart, and taking care not to deflate the dough.
4. Let the dough rest uncovered at room temperature until visibly puffy and jiggly when you gently shake the tray. (This may take 2 to 5 hours depending on the ambient room temperature.)

Bake and store the buns (20–25 minutes)

1. Preheat the oven to 500°F (260°C).
2. Bake the buns for 5 minutes, then reduce the temperature to 425°F (220°C) and bake for an additional 15 to 20 minutes or until the crust is deep golden and the internal temperature reads 190°F to 195°F (88°C to 91°C).
3. Let the buns cool on a wire rack before serving. These are best enjoyed the day they're baked but can be stored at room temperature in a resealable bag for up to 3 days or frozen in a freezer bag for up to 2 months.

Total time: 18–26 hours
Active prep time: 50 minutes
Baking time: 12–15 minutes
Makes: 10 English muffins

SPECIAL EQUIPMENT

Stand mixer fitted with a dough hook (optional)
Round 3½ to 4-inch (9 to 10cm) cookie cutter

INGREDIENTS

100g tap water
100g any type of milk (I use 2%)
167g active 100%-hydration sourdough starter
20g granulated sugar
1 medium egg
35g butter, softened
7g sea salt
355g white bread flour
Cornmeal, for dusting

English Muffins

Filled with fluffy nooks and crannies, these sourdough English muffins are a breakfast classic with a mild tang. They're perfect for slathering with a pat of butter or topping with a poached egg, and the subtle tang from the sourdough adds a depth of flavor without overwhelming the palate. This versatile breakfast bread is one you will come back to again and again.

Make and proof the dough (20 minutes active, 4–8 hours bulk proof at room temperature, overnight cold proof)

1. In a medium bowl or the bowl of a stand mixer, combine water, milk, starter, sugar, egg, salt, butter, and flour. Knead on low for 15 minutes until the dough becomes smooth and elastic. (Alternatively, you may knead the dough by hand for around 20 minutes.)
2. Cover the dough with a bowl cover or plastic wrap. Proof at room temperature until it has doubled in volume. (This may take 4 to 8 hours, depending on the ambient room temperature.) Place the covered dough in the refrigerator for an overnight cold proof.

Shape and final proof (15 minutes active, 2–6 hours final proof)

1. The next morning, prepare a baking sheet by lining it with parchment paper and generously dusting it with cornmeal.
2. Turn your dough out onto a lightly floured work surface. Using a rolling pin, roll the dough out to about ¾ inch (2cm) thick.
3. Using a round cutter, cut out as many English muffins as possible. Then gather the dough scraps, reroll the scraps into a single piece, and cut additional muffins. Continue until no dough remains. (You should have around 10 English muffins.) Place the muffins on the baking sheet.
4. Cover the muffins with a tea towel and allow them to proof at room temperature until nearly doubled in size and airy. (This may take 2 to 6 hours depending on the ambient room temperature.)

Cook and store the muffins (12–15 minutes)

1. Preheat a griddle or large skillet over medium heat. Lightly grease with butter or oil.
2. Carefully transfer the proofed muffins to the hot griddle or skillet. Cook for 5 to 7 minutes on each side or until golden brown and the internal temperature measures 195°F (91°C). Adjust heat as needed to prevent burning. Transfer the muffins to a wire rack to cool.
3. Store the cooled English muffins at room temperature in an airtight container or resealable bag for up to 3 days or freeze in a freezer bag for up to 2 months.

Total time: 15 hours
Active prep time: 30 minutes
Baking time: 20–25 minutes
Makes: 8 bagels

SPECIAL EQUIPMENT

Stand mixer fitted with a dough hook (optional)
Slotted spoon

INGREDIENTS

Dough

195g tap water
245g 100%-hydration sourdough starter (at peak)
75g honey
30g neutral oil (I use avocado oil)
11g sea salt
480g white bread flour

Boiling mixture

3L tap water
150g honey

Toppings

Roughly 10–12g of seeds per bagel (optional)

Montreal-Style Bagels

My homemade sourdough bagels have to be one of my favorite breads. With a whisper of honey—mimicking a Montreal-style bagel—and a very mellow sourdough tang, they are just perfect for a breakfast spread or a sandwich. This particular recipe does not call for a cold proof, which makes it one of my "faster" recipes. If you prepare the dough at night before bed, you can have sourdough bagels for lunch the next day!

Make and proof the dough (20 minutes active, 7–10 hour bulk proof at room temperature) (See Note)

1. In a medium bowl or the bowl of a stand mixer, combine the water, starter, honey, oil, salt, and flour. Knead on low or mix by hand for 15 to 20 minutes or until the dough is smooth and tacky.
2. Cover the bowl with a bowl cover or plastic wrap. Let the dough rise at room temperature for 7 to 10 hours or until the dough has doubled in size.

Shape and final proof (15 minutes active, 2–4 hour final proof)

1. Divide the dough into 8 equal-size portions and then roll each piece into a smooth ball.
2. To shape the bagels, make a small depression in the center of each ball using your thumb. Pinch through to create a hole, then gently stretch the dough outward in a circular motion until it resembles a bagel shape.
3. Place the shaped bagels on a parchment-lined baking tray and cover with a tea towel. Let them rise until nearly doubled in size. (This may take 2 to 4 hours depending on the ambient room temperature.)

Boil, bake, and store the bagels (25–35 minutes)

1. Preheat the oven to 400°F (205°C).
2. Bring 3 liters of water and 150 grams of honey to a gentle boil in a large pot. Prepare your seeds (if using) by placing them in a shallow bowl.
3. You will likely have to boil the bagels in batches, as you do not want to overcrowd your pot. (I usually boil two bagels at a time.) Using a slotted spoon, carefully lower a bagel into the boiling water. Cook the bagel for about 45 seconds on each side. Remove the bagel using the slotted spoon and place it into the seeds (if using), and then back on the parchment-lined baking tray. (Note: the bagels may appear quite wrinkly at this time.) Repeat the process with the remaining bagels.
4. Bake for 20 to 25 minutes or until the bagels are golden brown and the internal temperature reaches 200 to 205°F (93 to 96°C). Transfer to a wire rack to cool for at least 15 minutes.
5. Store the baked bagels at room temperature in a resealable bag for up to 3 days or freeze in an airtight container or freezer bag for up to 2 months.

Note:
You may wish to proof this dough overnight in order to have bagels in time for lunch the following day. If proofing overnight, consider using cool tap water to slow fermentation.

Total time: 7–30 hours
Active prep time: 45 minutes
Baking time: 15 minutes
Makes: 8 rolls

SPECIAL EQUIPMENT

Stand mixer fitted with a dough hook (optional)

INGREDIENTS

Dough

40g tap water
40g any type of milk (I use 2%)
225g 100%-hydration sourdough starter (at peak)
20g granulated sugar
6g sea salt
200g all-purpose flour
20g unsalted butter, softened and divided
Flaky sea salt (for sprinkling)

Filling

80g cold, unsalted butter divided into eight 2-inch (5cm) logs

Salt Butter Rolls (Shio Pan)

Crispy on the outside and pillowy soft on the inside, these salt butter rolls are the sourdough twist on the Japanese classic, known as *shio pan*. Tear into one of these rolls fresh out of the oven and you'll discover the delicious pocket of melted butter nestled at the center. They are perfect for breakfast, a savory snack, or to accompany a warm meal. This recipe is sure to be a hit in your family!

Prepare the dough (30 minutes, 3–7 hours proofing, optional overnight cold proof)

1. In the bowl of a stand mixer or a medium bowl, combine the water, milk, sourdough starter, sugar, salt, and flour. Knead on low or mix by hand until the dough comes together.
2. Add 10 grams of the butter, kneading on low in the stand mixer or mixing by hand until the butter is fully incorporated, then add the remaining 10 grams of butter. Knead for an additional 15 to 20 minutes or until the dough is smooth and elastic.
3. Cover the dough with a bowl cover or plastic wrap and let it proof until doubled in size. (This may take 3 to 7 hours, depending on room temperature.) Optionally, place the dough in the refrigerator for an overnight cold proof if you wish to delay baking.

Shape the dough (15 minutes, 1–6 hour final proof)

1. The next morning or after 3 to 7 hours, remove the dough from the bowl. Ensure the dough remains in a circular shape. If it has become misshapen, use your hands to form it into a circular disc. Using a bench scraper or knife, cut the dough straight through the center to divide it into two halves. Rotate the dough 90 degrees and cut through the center again, dividing it into four equal quarters. Finally, cut each quarter in half, giving you eight equal-size wedges.
2. Using a rolling pin, roll each triangle lengthwise until it is 11 inches (28cm) long and 3 inches (8cm) wide at the base.
3. Place a butter log at the base of the triangle, fold the dough over the sides of the butter, then roll up the dough. (You can slightly curve the shape of these so they form crescents, if you prefer.) Repeat with the remaining triangles. Place the shaped rolls on a parchment-lined baking sheet, with the seam at the bottom.
4. Cover the dough with a tea towel and let it rise until doubled and poofy and a finger-poke test produces a very slow return of the dough. If you have decided to bake these the same day, this may only take 1 to 2 hours. However, with an overnight cold proof, this will take anywhere from 2 to 6 hours depending on the ambient room temperature.

Bake and store (15 minutes)

1. Preheat the oven to 375°F (190°C).
2. Using a pastry brush, brush the tops of each roll with tap water and then sprinkle with flaky sea salt.
3. Bake for 15 minutes or until the tops are golden brown and the internal temperature measures 195°F (91°C). These rolls are best enjoyed warm and fresh out of the oven!
4. Store the baked rolls in an airtight container at room temperature for up to 2 days or freeze in a resealable bag for up to 3 months.

Total time: 30 hours
Active prep time: 55 minutes
Baking time: 15–17 minutes
Makes: 6 large or 8 medium rolls

SPECIAL EQUIPMENT

Stand mixer fitted with a dough hook (optional)
Bench scraper
Bread lame or razor blade

INGREDIENTS

225g any type of milk (I use 2%)
190g 100%-hydration active sourdough starter
25g granulated sugar
8g fine sea salt
400g all-purpose flour
40g unsalted butter, softened and divided
1 medium egg

Pain Viennois

Pain Viennois (Vienna bread), traditionally from Austria, is a soft, slightly sweet loaf that makes the perfect base for submarine sandwiches. Unlike your typical French baguette, this naturally leavened version has a tender crumb, a hint of sweetness, and a pillowy texture.

Make and proof the dough (25–30 minutes active, 4–10 hours bulk proof at room temperature, overnight cold proof)

1. In a medium bowl or the bowl of a stand mixer, combine the milk, starter, sugar, salt, and flour. Knead on low or mix by hand until fully combined, about 5 minutes.
2. Add half the butter and knead on low until fully combined. Add the remaining butter and knead on low for 20 minutes. (You may also knead the dough by hand for around 30 minutes instead.) Place the dough in a medium bowl and cover with a bowl cover or plastic wrap. Proof at room temperature until it has doubled in volume. (This may take 4 to 10 hours depending on the ambient room temperature.)
3. Place the covered dough in the refrigerator for an overnight cold proof.

Shape and final proof (10 minutes active, 3–8 hours final proof)

1. The next morning, prepare a baking sheet by lining it with parchment paper.
2. Turn the dough out onto a lightly floured surface and, using a bench scraper, divide it into six pieces for large-size rolls or eight pieces for medium-size rolls.
3. Flatten each dough piece and then, using your hands, roll it up into a log shape about 7 to 8 inches (18 to 20cm) long. Place each dough piece on the prepared baking sheet.
4. Whisk the egg in a small bowl. Brush the dough pieces with half the egg wash. Using a bread lame or razor blade, carefully score along each log about 10 to 15 times. Cover the dough loosely with plastic wrap and allow to proof until puffy and doubled in size. (This may take 3 to 8 hours depending on the ambient room temperature.)

Bake and store the rolls (15–17 minutes)

1. Preheat the oven to 450°F (230°C).
2. Brush the logs with the remaining egg wash. Bake for 15 to 17 minutes or until the internal temperature reaches 195°F (91°C). Let the rolls cool on a wire rack for 30 minutes before slicing.
3. Store the rolls at room temperature in a resealable bag for up to 3 days or freeze in an airtight container or freezer bag for up to 2 months.

German Soft Pretzels

Total time: 32 hours
Active prep time: 30–50 minutes
Baking time: 15–20 minutes
Makes: 10 pretzels

EQUIPMENT

Stand mixer fitted with a dough hook (optional)
Stainless-steel bowl (for the lye solution)
Slotted spoon
Latex or latex-free gloves
Protective eyewear

INGREDIENTS

225g tap water
200g 100%-hydration sourdough starter
25g light brown sugar
10g sea salt
50g unsalted butter, softened
500g bread flour

Lye solution

900g cool tap water
36g food-grade lye

Topping

Pretzel salt (optional)

Crispy, brown, and perfectly chewy, these sourdough pretzels are savory treats that are just as satisfying to make as they are to eat. The sourdough addition adds a depth of flavor and a mild tang. A quick dip in a lye solution is the secret to achieving the deep color and glossy finish.

Make and proof the dough (15 minutes active, 3–8 hours bulk proof at room-temperature, overnight cold proof)

1. In a medium bowl or the bowl of a stand mixer, combine the water, starter, sugar, salt, butter, and flour. Knead on low for 10 minutes. (You may knead the dough by hand for around 15 minutes instead.)
2. Cover the dough with a bowl cover or plastic wrap. Proof at room temperature until it has doubled in volume. (This may take 3 to 8 hours depending on the ambient room temperature.) Place the covered bowl in the refrigerator for an overnight cold proof.

Shape and final proof (20 minutes active, 2–6 hours final proofing)

1. The next morning, prepare a baking sheet by lining it with parchment paper or a silicone mat.
2. Turn the dough out onto a lightly floured surface. Using a bench scraper, divide the dough into ten equal-size portions that are about 100 grams each. Roll each piece into a long rope approximately 20 to 24 inches (51 to 61cm) in length, then shape as desired (traditional pretzels, sticks, or knots). Place the shaped dough, equally spaced, on the baking sheet.
3. Let the shaped pretzels proof uncovered at room temperature until puffy. (This may take 2 to 6 hours depending on the ambient room temperature.) Keeping the pretzels uncovered will help form a skin on the dough, which is crucial for achieving that distinctive pretzel crust.

***Prepare the lye solution and dip the pretzels (20 minutes active).* Important! Wear gloves and eye protection for these steps!**

1. Preheat the oven to 425°F (220°C). Put on your gloves and eye protection.
2. In a stainless-steel bowl, carefully dissolve the lye into the cool water. Stir gently until the lye is completely dissolved.
3. Using gloved hands, place each proofed pretzel into the lye solution for 15 to 20 seconds, ensuring all sides are submerged. Remove the pretzel with a slotted spoon and allow any excess solution to drip off before placing the pretzel back on the baking sheet. Repeat with the remaining pretzels.
4. Carefully pour the lye solution down the drain, rinse the bowl and spoon with cool water, and flush the lye down the drain with cool water.

Top, bake, and store the pretzels (15–20 minutes)

1. Sprinkle the pretzels with pretzel salt (if using). Bake for 15 to 20 minutes or until the pretzels are a deep golden brown and the internal temperature reaches 195°F (91°C). Allow to cool on a wire rack for 20 minutes.
2. Store at room temperature in a resealable bag for up to 2 days or freeze in an airtight container or freezer bag for up to 2 months.

Use caution with lye! Always wear gloves and eye protection when handling lye and work in a well-ventilated area. Take extra care to avoid splashing the lye, as it is caustic and can burn skin. When disposing of lye, carefully pour the solution slowly down the drain and flush with cool water.

Total time: 24–36 hours
Active prep time: 40–50 minutes
Baking time: 20 minutes
Makes: 6 simits

SPECIAL EQUIPMENT

Stand mixer fitted with a dough hook (optional)

INGREDIENTS

Dough

75g tap water
210g active 100%-hydration sourdough starter
60g honey
1 medium egg
15g neutral oil (I use avocado oil)
7g sea salt
320g white bread flour

Molasses water

70g tap water
70g fancy molasses

Toppings

150g sesame seeds

Turkish Simits

These chewy, sesame-crusted rings are a breakfast staple in Turkey. Similar to a bagel, the crunchy exterior is contrasted with the soft and mildly sweet crumb. And while Turkish simit are typically made with grape molasses, a good substitute—and the one called for in this recipe—is fancy molasses. Both flavors offer that distinctive sweetness and tang. Enjoy this simit with a cup of tea for breakfast or as a midday snack topped with feta, olives, and cucumbers!

Make and proof the dough (20 minutes active, 3–8 hours bulk proof at room temperature, overnight cold proof)

1. In a medium bowl or the bowl of a stand mixer, combine all the dough ingredients. Knead on low for 15 minutes or until the dough is smooth and elastic. (You may knead the dough by hand for around 20 minutes instead.)
2. Cover the dough with a bowl cover or plastic wrap. Proof at room temperature until it has doubled in volume. (This may take 3 to 8 hours depending on the ambient room temperature.) Place the covered dough in the refrigerator for an overnight cold proof.

Shape and final proof (20–30 minutes active, 3–6 hours final proof)

1. The next morning, prepare a baking sheet by lining it with parchment paper.
2. Turn the dough out onto a lightly floured surface. Use a bench scraper to divide the dough into twelve equal-size pieces. Roll each piece into an 18-inch (46cm) rope. Pair up the ropes, twist each pair together, then pinch the ends together to seal them into ring shapes.
3. Mix the water and molasses in a shallow bowl. Pour the sesame seeds into a separate bowl. Dip each ring into the molasses water, then immediately into the sesame seeds to coat thoroughly.
4. Place the rings on a parchment-lined baking sheet. Cover with plastic wrap and proof at room temperature until the simits are nearly doubled in size and a finger-poke test reveals a slow return of the dough.

Bake and store the simits (20 minutes)

1. Preheat the oven to 375°F (190°C).
2. Bake for 20 minutes or until deeply golden, browned on the bottoms, and the internal temperature reaches 200 to 205°F (93 to 96°C). Transfer to a wire rack to cool for at least 10 minutes.
3. These are best enjoyed the same day. Store simits at room temperature in a resealable bag for up to 2 days or freeze in an airtight container or freezer bag for up to 2 months.

CHAPTER 7

Flatbreads

Total time: 36 hours
Active prep time: 40 minutes
Baking time: 25–35 minutes
Makes: 1 focaccia

SPECIAL EQUIPMENT
One 9 × 13 × 2-inch (23 × 33 × 5cm) baking sheet

INGREDIENTS

Dough
400g tap water (375g if using all-purpose flour)
150g active 100%-hydration sourdough starter
25g honey
25g extra-virgin olive oil (plus more for drizzling and coating the pan)
10g sea salt
500g white bread flour (see Notes)

Toppings
Chopped fresh rosemary
Cherry tomatoes

Tomato-Rosemary Focaccia

One of my most well-loved recipes is this absolutely divine focaccia. Whether you are well-versed at sourdough baking or brand new to it, this simple recipe is a surefire showstopper. It produces a beautiful, airy dough with a crispy, olive-oil infused exterior. And while I prefer to eat this versatile bread on its own, it can be used to make a delicious sandwich!

Make and proof the dough (25 minutes active, 3–4 hours rest, 6–19 hours cold proof)

1. In a medium mixing bowl, combine the water, starter, honey, olive oil, salt, and flour. Mix by hand or with a dough whisk until fully incorporated. Cover with a bowl cover or plastic wrap and let rest for 45 minutes.
2. Perform a coil fold (p. 35). Cover and let rest for another 30 to 45 minutes.
3. Perform three to four coil folds in intervals of 45 minutes, covering the dough between folds.
4. Transfer the dough to the refrigerator and let it chill for at least for 6 hours and up to 19 hours.

Shape and final proof (5 minutes active, 6–10 hours final proof)

1. Line the baking sheet with parchment paper and generously coat it with 15 to 20 grams of olive oil.
2. Remove the dough from the refrigerator. Using a coil-fold technique, slide your fingers under the dough and transfer the dough to the prepared pan. Cover the dough with plastic wrap and let it proof at room temperature until it has at least doubled in size, appears airy, and jiggles when the pan is gently shaken from side to side. (This may take 6 to 10 hours depending on the ambient room temperature.)

Bake and store the focaccia (25–35 minutes)

1. Preheat your oven to 435°F (225°C).
2. Drizzle olive oil over the surface of the dough. Use your fingers to press dimples into the dough all the way to the bottom of the pan. Insert fresh rosemary and whole cherry tomatoes into the dimples.
3. Bake for 25 to 35 minutes or until the internal temperature reaches 195°F (91°C).
4. Remove the focaccia from the oven and the sheet/parchment paper, and place it directly on a cooling rack. (Removing it from the pan and parchment paper ensures the bottom will remain crispy.) Let it cool for at least 45 minutes before slicing.
5. Store at room temperature in a resealable bag for up to 3 days or freeze in an airtight container or freezer bag for up to 2 months.

Notes:
Be sure to use a high-protein bread flour (>12.5% protein content), as this will ensure the flour is able to fully absorb all the water without the dough becoming soupy. If you are only able to find all-purpose flour, reduce the water content to 375 grams.

I typically mix the dough in the morning and complete all folds by around 1 p.m., then put the dough in the refrigerator until about 10 p.m. I then pull the dough out, transfer it to the baking sheet, cover it with plastic wrap, and let it proof at room temperature overnight. It is usually fully proofed by the morning, making it perfect for breakfast or brunch!

Total time: 24–36 hours
Active prep time: 40 minutes
Baking time: 35–40 minutes
Makes: 1 focaccia

SPECIAL EQUIPMENT

One 9 × 13 × 2-inch (23 × 33 × 5cm) baking sheet

INGREDIENTS

Dough

400g tap water (375g if using all-purpose flour)
150g active 100%-hydration sourdough starter
70g honey
25g unsalted butter, melted (plus more for drizzling and coating the pan)
10g sea salt
500g white bread flour (see Notes)

Toppings

2 medium Honeycrisp apples, peeled and diced into ½-inch (1.25cm) cubes or thinly sliced
70g granulated sugar
6g ground cinnamon

Apple-Cinnamon Focaccia

This focaccia combines warm spiced apples with a beautiful bubbly dough. This cozy, fragrant bread has a crispy bottom from the generous drizzle of olive oil and a soft, airy crumb. It's perfect for breakfast, a midday snack, or eaten à la mode for dessert!

Make and proof the dough (25 minutes active, 3–4 hours rest, 6–19 hours cold proof)

1. In a medium mixing bowl, combine the water, starter, honey, butter, salt, and flour. Mix by hand or with a dough whisk until fully incorporated. Cover with a bowl cover or plastic wrap and let rest for 45 minutes.
2. Perform a coil fold (p. 35). Cover and rest for another 45 minutes.
3. Perform three to four coil folds in intervals of 45 minutes, covering the dough between folds.
4. Transfer the dough to the refrigerator and let it chill for at least for 6 hours or up to 19 hours.

Shape and final proof (5 minutes active, 6–10 hours final proof)

1. Line the baking pan with parchment paper and generously coat the paper with 15 to 20 grams of melted butter.
2. Remove the dough from the refrigerator. Using a coil-fold technique, slide your fingers under the dough and transfer the dough to the prepared pan. Cover the dough with plastic wrap and let it proof at room temperature until it has at least doubled in size, appears airy, and jiggles when the pan is gently shaken from side to side. (This may take 6 to 10 hours depending on the ambient room temperature.)

Bake and store the focaccia (35–40 minutes)

1. Preheat the oven to 400°F (205°C).
2. In a small bowl, combine the cinnamon and sugar. Mix until thoroughly combined.
3. Drizzle melted butter over the surface of the dough. Use your fingers to press dimples into the dough all the way to the bottom of the pan. Sprinkle the cinnamon-sugar mixture over the top and then sprinkle the apples on top of that. Dimple the dough again with your fingers.
4. Bake for 35 to 40 minutes or until the internal temperature of the dough reaches 195°F (91°C).
5. Remove the focaccia from the oven and the baking sheet, and place it directly on a cooling rack. (Removing it from the pan and parchment paper ensures the bottom will remain crispy.) Let it cool for at least 45 minutes before slicing and serving.
6. Store at room temperature in a resealable bag for up to 3 days or in an airtight container or freezer bag for up to 2 months.

Notes:

Be sure to use a high-protein bread flour (>12.5% protein content), as this will ensure the flour is able to fully absorb all the water without the dough becoming soupy. If you are only able to find all-purpose flour, reduce the water content to 375 grams.

I typically mix the dough in the morning and complete all folds by around 1 p.m., then put the dough in the refrigerator until about 10 p.m. I then pull the dough out, transfer it to the baking sheet, cover it with plastic wrap, and let it proof at room temperature overnight. It is usually fully proofed by the morning, making it perfect for breakfast or brunch!

Total time: 24–36 hours
Active prep time: 40 minutes
Baking time: 35–40 minutes
Makes: 1 focaccia

SPECIAL EQUIPMENT
One 9 × 13 × 2-inch (23 × 33 × 5cm) baking sheet

INGREDIENTS

Dough
400g tap water (375g if using all-purpose flour)
150g active 100%-hydration sourdough starter
65g honey
25g extra-virgin olive oil (plus more for drizzling and coating the pan)
10g sea salt
500g white bread flour

Toppings
3 fresh peaches, sliced (you can substitute sliced, canned peaches)
85g goat cheese, crumbled
4–5 sprigs fresh thyme, leaves removed and stems discarded
25g honey

Peach and Goat Cheese Focaccia

Also known as my "big bubble focaccia," this airy crumb has a crispy exterior and vibrant toppings that combine to produce a pleasure for the senses. Juicy, fresh peaches and creamy goat cheese create a beautiful sweet-and-savory combination that is so pleasing to the palate. Whether served for breakfast or as a side for a summer party, this focaccia is sure to be enjoyed by all!

Make and proof the dough (25 minutes active, 3–4 hours rest, 6–19 hours cold proof)

1. In a medium mixing bowl, combine the water, starter, honey, olive oil, salt, and flour. Mix by hand or with a dough whisk until fully incorporated. Cover with a bowl cover or plastic wrap and let rest for 45 minutes.
2. Perform a coil fold (p. 35). Cover let rest for another 45 minutes.
3. Perform three to four coil folds in intervals of 45 minutes, covering the dough between folds.
4. Transfer the dough to the refrigerator and let it chill for at least for 6 hours and up to 19 hours.

Shape and final proof (5 minutes active, 6–10 hours final proof)

1. Line the baking sheet with parchment paper and generously coat it with 15 to 20 grams of olive oil.
2. Remove the dough from the refrigerator. Using a coil-fold technique, slide your fingers under the dough and transfer the dough to the prepared pan. Cover the dough with plastic wrap and let it proof at room temperature until it has at least doubled in size, appears airy, and jiggles when the pan is gently shaken from side to side. (This may take 6 to 10 hours depending on the ambient room temperature.)

Bake and store the focaccia (35–40 minutes)

1. Preheat the oven to 400°F (205°C).
2. Drizzle olive oil over the surface of the dough. Use your fingers to press dimples into the dough all the way to the bottom of the pan.
3. Place the peach slices, crumbled goat cheese, and thyme leaves evenly across the dough, and then dock/dimple the dough again with your fingers.
4. Bake for 35 to 40 minutes or until the bread is deeply golden and the internal temperature reaches 195°F (91°C).
5. Remove the focaccia from the oven and the baking sheet and place it directly on a cooling rack. (Removing it from the pan and parchment paper ensures the bottom remains crispy.) Drizzle the dough with 25 grams of honey while it is cooling. Let it cool for at least 45 minutes before slicing and serving.
6. Store the bread at room temperature in a resealable bag for up to 3 days or freeze for up to 2 months in an airtight container or freezer bag.

Notes:
Be sure to use a high-protein bread flour (>12.5% protein content), as this will ensure the flour is able to fully absorb all the water without the dough becoming soupy. If you are only able to find all-purpose flour, reduce the water content to 375 grams.

I typically mix the dough in the morning and complete all folds by around 1 p.m., then put the dough in the refrigerator until about 10 p.m. I then pull the dough out, transfer it to the baking pan, cover it with plastic wrap, and let it proof at room temperature overnight. It is usually fully proofed by the morning, making it perfect for breakfast or brunch!

Total time: 32–48 hours
Active prep time: 30 minutes
Baking time: 35–40 minutes
Makes: 1 Pala Romana

SPECIAL EQUIPMENT

One 13 × 18-inch (33 × 45.75cm) baking sheet

INGREDIENTS

350g tap water
170g 100%-hydration active sourdough starter
25g extra-virgin olive oil
10g sea salt
500g bread flour
Corn flour (cornmeal) for sprinkling

Pala Romana

This delicious flatbread has an airy, open crumb and a crisp, golden, cornmeal-dusted crust. Typically baked as one large slab, it can be sliced and enjoyed as a sandwich or even on its own. The ease with which this recipe is made is sure to make it a regular in your baking regime.

Make and proof the dough (20 minutes active, 4–8 hours bulk proof, overnight cold proof)

1. Combine all the dough ingredients except the corn flour in a medium mixing bowl and mix by hand or with a dough whisk until well combined. Cover with a bowl cover or plastic wrap and let the dough rest for 30 to 45 minutes.
2. After the allotted time has elapsed, perform a stretch-and-fold (p. 34). Cover and let the dough rest for 30 to 45 minutes.
3. Over the next 3 to 4 hours, perform three sets of coil folds (p. 35) spaced 30 to 45 minutes apart. Cover and let the dough bulk proof at room temperature until it has nearly doubled in size. (This may take 4 to 8 hours depending on the ambient room temperature.) Place the covered dough in the refrigerator for an overnight cold proof.

Shape and final proof (5 minutes active, 4–8 hours final proof)

1. The next morning, prepare a baking sheet by lining it with parchment paper and sprinkling it liberally with corn flour.
2. Using a coil-fold technique, transfer the dough from the bowl to the baking sheet. Cover the dough with plastic wrap and let it rest at room temperature until the dough has doubled in size, appears airy, and is very jiggly when the cookie sheet is gently shaken from side to side. (This may take 4 to 8 hours depending on the ambient room temperature.)

Bake and store the Pala Romana (5 minutes active, 35–40 minutes bake)

1. Preheat the oven to 425°F (220°C).
2. Remove the plastic wrap from the dough and lightly sprinkle the top with corn flour.
3. Using your fingers, dock the dough by pressing your fingers into it until you reach the bottom of the pan. (If you want to add toppings, you should add them now.)
4. Place the dough in the oven and bake for 35 to 40 minutes or until the internal temperature measures 195°F (91°C).
5. Transfer the dough to a wire rack and allow it to cool for 45 minutes before slicing.
6. Store the bread at room temperature in a resealable bag for up to 3 days or freeze for up to 2 months in an airtight container or freezer bag.

Total time: 5–7 hours
Active prep time: 55 minutes
Baking time: 3–4 minutes per naan
Makes: 6–8 naan

SPECIAL EQUIPMENT

Stand mixer fitted with a dough hook (optional)
Cast-iron skillet or heavy frying pan

INGREDIENTS

Dough

65g tap water
200g 100%-hydration active sourdough starter
15g granulated sugar
60g plain Greek-style yogurt (I use 1% milk fat)
22g extra-virgin olive oil
6g sea salt
250g all-purpose flour

Toppings

Melted butter (optional)
Herbs (optional)
Garlic (optional)

Same-Day Sourdough Naan

This soft and fluffy naan is naturally leavened with a generous amount of sourdough starter, allowing it to ferment quickly and be ready the same day. The addition of yogurt gives it that signature tang you'd expect from an authentic naan. My son calls this the best bread I've ever made, and honestly, it's one of my favorites too—not just for its tender texture and delicious flavor, but for how effortlessly it comes together in a single day. It's perfect for scooping up curries, dips, or enjoying on its own.

Mix and proof the dough (15 minutes active, 3–5 hours bulk proof at room temperature)

1. In a medium bowl or the bowl of a stand mixer, combine all dough ingredients. Knead on low for 6 to 7 minutes or until the dough becomes smooth and elastic. (You may knead the dough by hand for 10 minutes instead.)
2. Cover the dough with a bowl cover or plastic wrap and let it rise in a warm spot until it has doubled in size and is visibly puffy. (This may take 3 to 5 hours depending on the ambient room temperature.)

Shape and rest the dough (20 minutes active, 1.5 hours rest)

1. Turn the dough out onto a lightly floured surface. Use a bench scraper to divide the dough into six to eight equal-size portions (about 75 to 100 grams each). Shape each portion into a ball.
2. Cover the dough balls with a tea towel and let them rest for 1 hour to relax the gluten, making them easier to roll out.
3. On a lightly floured surface, use a rolling pin to roll out each ball into an oval or circle about 6 to 8 inches (15 to 20cm) across and ⅕ inch (5mm) thick. Alternatively, if you find the dough too sticky, you can hand-pull the dough balls into ovals. Let them rest for 20 to 30 minutes.

Cook and store the naan (20 minutes)

1. Heat a cast-iron skillet or heavy frying pan over medium heat.
2. Gently stretch a naan round into an oblong shape, then place the dough onto the hot skillet. Cook for 1 to 2 minutes or until bubbles form and the underside has golden brown spots. Flip and cook for another 1 to 2 minutes.
3. Optionally, brush with melted butter and sprinkle with herbs or garlic after cooking. Serve warm.
4. Store any leftovers in an airtight container at room temperature for up to 2 days or freeze for up to 1 month in an airtight container or freezer bag.

Total time: 24–36 hours
Active prep time: 1 hour 20 minutes
Baking time: 1–2 minutes per pita in a pizza oven; 3–4 minutes per pita in a conventional oven
Makes: 12 pitas

SPECIAL EQUIPMENT

Stand mixer fitted with a dough hook (optional)
Open-ended nonstick cookie sheet or pizza peel
Pizza oven or baking stone, baking steel, or heavy baking sheet (for baking in a conventional oven)

INGREDIENTS

315g tap water
100g 100%-hydration active sourdough starter
17g extra-virgin olive oil
12g sea salt
450g white bread flour
125g whole wheat flour

Pocket Pitas

These soft pocket pitas are a joy to make and even more satisfying to tear into. Naturally leavened with sourdough starter, they have a subtle tang and wonderful chew. They're perfect for stuffing to the brim with grilled meats, vegetables, and spreads, or for tearing and dipping into your favorite dips and sauces.

Prepare the dough (15 minutes active, 4–8 hours bulk proof at room temperature, overnight cold proof)

1. In a medium bowl or the bowl of a stand mixer, combine all ingredients. Knead on low for 10 minutes until the dough becomes smooth and elastic. (Alternatively, you may knead the dough by hand for 15 minutes.)
2. Cover the bowl with a bowl cover or plastic wrap. Proof at room temperature until it has doubled in volume. (This may take 4 to 8 hours, depending on the ambient room temperature.) Place the covered dough in the refrigerator for an overnight cold proof.

Divide and final proof (10 minutes active, 2–5 hours final proof)

1. The next morning, use a bench scraper to divide your dough into twelve equal-size portions and then shape each into a ball.
2. Cover the balls with a tea towel and allow to proof at room temperature until doubled in size. (This may take 2 to 5 hours depending on the ambient room temperature.)

Roll out, bake and store the pitas (50–60 minutes active)

1. Preheat a pizza oven to 700°F (370°C) or a conventional oven to 500°F (260°C) with a baking stone, baking steel, or heavy baking sheet placed on the middle rack.
2. On a lightly floured surface, roll each ball into a 7- to 8-inch (18 to 20cm) circle that is approximately ¼ inch (6mm) thick.
3. ***For a pizza oven:*** Use a pizza peel to slide a pita round into the oven. Bake for roughly 2 minutes or until the pita puffs up and develops golden-brown spots, rotating frequently with a circular pizza peel to ensure even baking. Repeat with remaining pitas.
4. ***For a conventional oven:*** Use an open-ended baking sheet to place one pita round directly onto the hot baking surface in the oven. Bake for 3 to 4 minutes or until the pita puffs up and is lightly browned. Repeat with remaining pitas.
5. Cool the pitas for a few minutes on a wire rack.
6. Serve warm or store in an airtight container at room temperature for up to 3 days or freeze in an airtight container or freezer bag for up to 2 months.

Note:
For best results, use a preheated baking stone, baking steel, or heavy baking sheet to mimic the high heat of a pizza oven, which helps the pitas puff up properly.

Total time: 32 hours
Active prep time: 20 minutes
Baking time: 20–25 minutes
Makes: Three 9-inch (23cm) round pides

INGREDIENTS

Dough
230g warm tap water
230g any type of milk (I use 2%)
220g 100%-hydration active sourdough starter
17g maple syrup or honey
1 medium egg white (reserve the yolk for the next day)
30g extra-virgin olive oil
15g sea salt
700g white bread flour

Spread
1 medium egg yolk (reserved from the previous day)
30g plain Greek yogurt
3g sea salt

Fluffy Turkish Pides

These Middle Eastern flatbreads feature fluffy, airy interiors and golden crusts. With the slow fermentation of sourdough, the enhanced flavor profile is sure to be enjoyed by all. These can be topped with savory spices, seeds, herbs, cheeses, or meats. The versatility of these flatbreads makes them a perfect addition to any meal.

Make and proof the dough (15 minutes active, 3–8 hours bulk proof at room temperature, overnight cold proof)

1. In a medium mixing bowl, combine all dough ingredients. Mix by hand or with a dough whisk until fully incorporated. Cover with a bowl cover or plastic wrap and let rest for 30 minutes.
2. Perform a stretch-and-fold (p. 34). Cover and rest for 1 hour.
3. Perform three coil folds (p. 35) over the next 2 hours, covering the dough between folds.
4. Let the dough rise at room temperature until it has doubled in size. Place the covered dough in the refrigerator for an overnight cold proof. (This may take 3 to 8 hours depending on the ambient room temperature.)

Shape and final proof (5 minutes active, 2–8 hours final proof)

1. The next morning, prepare two baking sheets by lining them with parchment paper.
2. Remove the dough from the fridge and lightly flour your work surface. Using a bench scraper or sharp knife, divide the dough into three equal-size pieces and then shape the pieces into balls. Using your hands, flatten each ball into a 9-inch (23cm) disc and place two on one cookie sheet and the third on the second baking sheet. Cover the discs with a cotton tea towel and let them rise until they are puffy and a finger-poke test reveals a slow return of the dough. (This may take 2 to 8 hours depending on the ambient room temperature.)

Bake and store the pides (20–25 minutes)

1. Preheat the oven to 400°F (205°C).
2. In a small bowl, whisk together the spread ingredients until cohesive.
3. Spread the mixture onto the discs and dimple (dock) the dough using your fingers to create a checkered pattern. (If desired, you can add seeds, herbs, spices, ground meat, or cheeses of your choice.)
4. Bake the discs for 20 to 25 minutes or until golden brown and puffy and the internal temperature measures 195°F (91°C).
5. Store in an airtight container for up to 5 days at room temperature (or in the refrigerator if topped with meat or cheese). Freeze in a freezer bag for up to 2 months.

Total time: 36 hours
Active prep time: 45 minutes
Baking time: 2–12 minutes (depending on the oven type)
Makes: Four 12-inch (30cm) pizzas

SPECIAL EQUIPMENT

Pizza stone or baking steel
Open-ended nonstick cookie sheet
Pizza oven (optional)
Pizza peel (if using a pizza oven)

INGREDIENTS

375g tap water
150g 100%-hydration active sourdough starter
10g sea salt
500g bread flour
Semolina flour or corn flour (for shaping)

Neapolitan-Style Sourdough Pizzas

Rival your favorite Italian pizzeria with these delightful, airy, Neapolitan-style pizzas! Whether you're using a pizza oven or a traditional oven, this recipe takes you through the process of achieving a golden, crispy base, with a light and airy cornicione (crust). Your pizza-loving pals will be lining up for more!

Make and proof the dough (15 minutes active, 3–6 hours bulk proof at room temperature, overnight cold proof [to further to enhance the flavor and texture of the dough, cold proof the dough overnight twice])

1. Combine all the dough ingredients in a medium bowl. Mix by hand until a shaggy dough forms. Cover with a bowl cover or plastic wrap and let it rest for 30 to 45 minutes.
2. After the allotted time has elapsed, perform a stretch-and-fold (p. 34). Cover and let the dough rest for 30 to 45 minutes more.
3. Perform three coil folds (p. 35) at 30- to 45-minute intervals, covering the dough between folds. After the coil folds are complete, cover the dough and place it in the refrigerator for one overnight cold proof or two overnight cold proofs.

Preshape and final proof the dough (10 minutes, 3–8 hours proof at room temperature) (see Note)

1. The next day or the one following, liberally flour a flat tray. (The tray does not need to be oven safe.)
2. Turn the dough out onto a well-floured surface and, using a bench scraper, divide the dough into four equal-size portions and shape them into balls. Place the balls on the tray and cover with a tea towel.
3. Let the dough balls proof at room temperature until doubled in size. (This may take 3 to 8 hours depending on the ambient room temperature.)

Shape the dough (20 minutes)

1. Preheat a pizza oven to 700°F (370°C) or a conventional oven to 500°F (260°C).
2. Liberally dust the work surface with with semolina flour or corn flour to prevent sticking. Place a dough ball onto the surface and gently press down into the dough using your fingertips, working outward in a circular motion, leaving about ¾ inch (2cm) of the edge untouched to form the cornicione (crust).
3. Begin stretching the dough by picking it up and draping it over the backs of your hands, keeping your fists under the dough. Slowly rotate the dough in a circular motion, letting its own weight stretch it evenly. (Be gentle and swift to avoid tearing.) If you prefer, you may lay the dough onto the floured surface and stretch it gently with your full, flat hand, working outward from the center. Stretch the dough into a 12-inch (30cm) diameter circle. Repeat with the remaining dough balls.
4. Gently transfer one pizza base to a pizza peel or a baking sheet lined with parchment paper by lightly dragging it from one side and then gently reshaping it into a circular shape. (This will also help to stretch the dough further)

Bake and store the pizzas (2 minutes per pizza in a pizza oven, 10–14 minutes per pizza in a conventional oven)

1. ***Optional step:*** If desired, you can par-bake the crusts. Brush the pizza base with olive oil and bake in a pizza oven or traditional oven for a few minutes without the toppings. This will help dry the bottom of the crust, since a pizza that is overloaded with toppings can develop a soggy bottom when baked.

2. ***For a pizza oven:*** Add any desired toppings and bake for roughly 2 minutes per pizza, rotating frequently with a circular pizza peel.
3. ***For a conventional oven:*** Add desired toppings, bake for 5 to 7 minutes per pizza, then remove and add more toppings, if desired. Bake for an additional 5 to 7 minutes.
4. Store in a sealed container in the refrigerator for up to 5 days or in the freezer for up to 2 months.
5. To reheat a cooked pizza, preheat your conventional oven to 375°F (190°C). Bake on a parchment paper-lined baking sheet for 5 to 10 minutes or until the cheese is melted and the crust begins to brown.

Note:
Depending on when you want to eat the pizzas, you should take into consideration the fact that the dough will proof a lot faster in a warmer environment. If the temperature in your home is between 75°F and 79°F (24°C and 26°C), I would recommend pre-shaping the dough about 4 hours before you want to serve the pizzas. However, if the temperature in your home is cooler and between 66°F and 74°F (19°C and 23°C), you should consider preshaping the dough earlier in the day to allow the dough to proof fully.

Total time: 18–26 hours
Active prep time: 45 minutes
Baking time: 8–12 minutes
Makes: Two 12-inch (30cm) rounds

SPECIAL EQUIPMENT

Stand mixer fitted with a dough hook (optional)
Pizza stone or baking steel
Open-ended nonstick cookie sheet or pizza peel
Pizza oven (optional)

INGREDIENTS

Dough

250g tap water
150g active 100%-hydration sourdough starter
20g honey
20g extra-virgin olive oil
7g sea salt
350g white bread flour

Toppings

50g unsalted butter
3–4 cloves of garlic, minced
Pinch of salt
280g grated mozzarella cheese

Donair sauce

70g sweetened condensed milk
30g white vinegar
2g garlic powder

Garlic Fingers with Donair Sauce

A late-night classic from the east coast of Canada, Garlic Fingers with Donair Sauce is the ultimate combination of chewy, savory, and a touch of sweet. I first had them as a student at Mount Allison University—boxes of garlic fingers and sweet donair sauce were practically a rite of passage. This sourdough version brings all that nostalgia, with a chewy golden crust and that signature garlicky flavor. Pair them with the sweet donair sauce (definitely an acquired taste!) or keep it simple and serve them with marinara sauce.

Make and proof the dough (20 minutes active, 4–8 hours bulk proof at room temperature, overnight cold proof)

1. In a medium bowl or the bowl of a stand mixer, combine all dough ingredients. Knead on low for 15 minutes. (Alternatively, you may knead the dough by hand for around 20 minutes.)
2. Cover the dough with a bowl cover or plastic wrap. Proof at room temperature until it has doubled in volume. (This may take 4 to 8 hours depending on the ambient room temperature.) Place the covered dough in the refrigerator for an overnight cold proof.

Shape and final proof (15 minutes active, 2–6 hours final proof)

1. The next day, lightly flour your work surface. Divide the dough into two equal-size pieces and shape them into balls.
2. Cover the dough balls with a tea towel or plastic wrap and allow them to proof at room temperature until nearly doubled in size and airy. (This may take 2 to 6 hours depending on the ambient room temperature.)

Make the garlic-butter topping and donair sauce (5 minutes active)

1. Preheat a pizza oven to 700°F (370°C) or a conventional oven to 500°F (260°C) with pizza stone or baking steel placed inside the oven.
2. Prepare the garlic-butter topping by melting the butter in a saucepan and then adding the garlic and salt. Sauté the garlic for 1 minute and then remove the saucepan from the heat and set it aside.
3. Prepare the donair sauce by mixing all of the ingredients in a small bowl.

Shape the dough (10 minutes)

1. Lightly flour your work surface. Place a dough ball onto the surface and gently press down into the dough using your fingertips, working outward in a circular motion all the way to the edge of the dough.
2. Begin stretching the dough by picking it up and draping it over the backs of your hands, keeping your fists under the dough. Slowly rotate the dough in a circular motion, letting its own weight stretch it evenly. (Be gentle and swift to avoid tearing.) Stretch the dough into a 12-inch (30cm) diameter circle. Repeat with the remaining dough ball.
3. Gently transfer the dough to the pizza peel or an open-ended nonstick cookie sheet by lightly dragging one side. (This will also help to stretch the dough further.) Lightly reshape it into a circular shape once it's on the sheet or peel.
4. Brush each round with the garlic-butter topping and then top with the shredded mozzarella.

Bake and store (8–12 minutes)

1. Bake in a pizza oven for roughly 2 minutes, rotating frequently with a circular pizza peel, or bake in a conventional oven for 8 to 12 minutes, until the crust is puffed and golden brown and the cheese has melted.
2. Store in a sealed container in the fridge for up to 5 days or in the freezer for up to 2 months. Reheat in the oven for 10 minutes at 350°F (175°C).

Total time:
1 hour 30 minutes
Active prep time:
30 minutes
Baking time: 12–18 minutes
Makes: 12 tortillas

SPECIAL EQUIPMENT

Stand mixer fitted with a dough hook (optional)
Large cast-iron pan or skillet

INGREDIENTS

125g tap water
125g 100%-hydration sourdough starter (active or discard)
35g unsalted butter, softened
7g sea salt
250g all-purpose flour

Soft Tortillas

These soft, chewy, sourdough tortillas come together with minimal kneading and fermentation time, making them perfect for last-minute meals or weeknight dinners. Whether you load them up with your favorite burrito fillings, turn them into quesadillas, or tear them up to scoop your go-to dips, they're endlessly versatile—and far better than anything store bought.

Make the dough and shape into balls (5–10 minutes active, 30–60 minutes rest)

1. In a medium bowl or bowl of the stand mixer, combine all ingredients. Knead on low for 5 minutes or until a cohesive dough forms and it is no longer sticking to the surface of the bowl. (You may knead the dough by hand for around 10 minutes instead.)
2. Remove the dough from the bowl and, using a bench scraper, divide the dough into twelve equal-size pieces and then shape the pieces into balls. Cover the balls with plastic wrap and let them rest for 30 to 60 minutes to allow the gluten to relax and to make rolling easier.

Shape the tortillas (20 minutes active)

1. Dust a ball lightly with flour and, using a rolling pin and without tearing the dough, roll it out as thinly as possible into a circle that is around 10 to 11 inches (25 to 28cm).
2. Place a square of parchment paper on top of each tortilla and then place the next tortilla on top of the last.

Cook and store the tortillas (12–18 minutes)

1. Heat the cast-iron pan on medium-high heat. (No oil is required.)
2. Gently place a tortilla in the center of the pan and cook until it starts to puff up and brown on the bottom. Carefully flip the tortilla with tongs or a fork and cook until the underside becomes brown in spots. Each tortilla will take around 1 to 1½ minutes to cook.
3. You may stack the tortillas, wrap them in tin foil, and place them in the oven set to 200°F (95°C) to keep them warm.
4. Store the tortillas in an airtight container at room temperature for up to 5 days or freeze in an airtight container or freezer bag for up to 2 months.

Total time: about 4 hours
Active prep time: 2 hours 15 minutes
Baking time: 1 hour (5 minutes per msemen)
Makes: 12 msemen

INGREDIENTS

345g tap water
180g 100%-hydration active sourdough starter
20g granulated sugar
8g fine sea salt
265g all-purpose flour
325g fine semolina, plus extra for layering
40g unsalted butter, melted
40g neutral oil (I use avocado oil)

Moroccan-Style Msemen

These buttery, flaky flatbreads are breakfast staples in Morocco. Traditionally eaten with honey or jam, they also pair perfectly with a hot cup of mint tea. My sourdough version adds a subtle tang while making excellent use of extra sourdough starter. Try them out for a simple and relatively quick sourdough bread.

Make and rest the dough (15 minutes active, 50–90 minutes rest)

1. In a medium bowl, combine the water, sourdough starter, sugar, salt, flour, and semolina. Mix by hand or with a dough whisk or wooden spoon until the dough comes together. Knead the dough for about 10 minutes or until smooth and elastic. Cover the dough with a bowl cover or plastic wrap and let it rest for 30 to 60 minutes.
2. Use a bench scraper to divide the dough into twelve equal-size portions that are approximately 94 grams each. Roll each portion into a smooth ball.
3. Lightly brush the balls with oil to prevent a skin from forming. Cover with a tea towel and rest for 20 to 30 minutes.

Shape the dough (1 hour active, 30 minutes rest)

1. Melt the butter and combine it with the oil in a small bowl. To another bowl, add some semolina flour.
2. Generously coat your hands and work surface with the butter-oil mixture. Gently flatten one dough ball, then use your fingers to coax it outward into an 11-inch (28cm) square. If the dough resists or tears, let it rest an additional 20 minutes.
3. Once the dough is stretched thin (but not torn), brush it generously with the butter-oil mixture and sprinkle it lightly with semolina.
4. Fold the dough into thirds, like a letter, adding more butter-oil mixture and semolina between layers. Fold it into thirds again in the opposite direction to create a small square. Repeat with the remaining dough balls. Cover with a tea towel and allow the squares to rest for an additional 30 minutes.
5. Once 30 minutes has elapsed, take one prepared square and use your fingers to gently press it into an 8-inch (20cm) square. Repeat with the remaining dough. (You may make a stack of these since the butter-oil mixture will prevent sticking.)

Cook and store the msemen (1 hour or 4–6 minutes per msemen)

1. Heat a cast-iron skillet or nonstick pan over medium heat. Add a small amount of butter to the pan.
2. Cook each msemen for 2 to 3 minutes on one side, then flip and cook an additional 2 to 3 minutes until golden and flaky. Place the cooked msemen on a wire rack to cool and repeat with the remaining msemen.
3. Store at room temperature in an airtight container or resealable bag for up to 2 days or freeze in an airtight container or freezer bag for up to 2 months. Reheat in a warm skillet.

Total time: 5 hours
Active prep time:
1 hour 35 minutes
Baking time: 1 hour
(5 minutes per paratha)
Makes: 12 paratha

INGREDIENTS
350g all-purpose flour
9g sea salt
200g warm tap water
105g 100%-hydration sourdough starter (active or discard)
19g neutral oil (I use avocado oil)
170g butter, melted and divided

Buttery Paratha

Paratha are delicious flatbreads known for being a cherished staple in many Indian households. And while paratha wasn't typically on the menu in my grandmother's home, it became a fast favorite of mine with its buttery layers and tender chew. This sourdough version brings a subtle tang thanks to the discard in the dough. Try them when you want something comforting, simple, and endlessly versatile.

Make the dough (5 minutes active, 30 minutes rest)

1. Whisk the flour and salt in a large bowl.
2. In a small bowl, whisk together the warm water and sourdough starter until fully incorporated.
3. Make a well in the flour and add the starter mixture and the oil.
4. Mix by hand until fully combined. (There is no need to knead it for more than a few minutes.) Cover with a bowl cover or plastic wrap and rest for 30 minutes.

Shape and rest the dough (15 minutes active, 1–3 hours rest)

1. Place the dough onto a lightly floured work surface. Using a bench scraper, divide it into twelve equal-size pieces and then shape each piece into a ball. Cover the balls with plastic wrap and set them aside to rest for 30 minutes.
2. After 30 minutes, lightly dust a dough ball and use a rolling pin to roll it out into a 10-inch (25cm) square, or make it as thin as it will go without tearing the dough, dusting with flour to prevent sticking.
3. Place a tablespoon of the melted butter on each square and spread it evenly, all the way to the edges of the dough.
4. Roll the dough up from the bottom and coil it up to form a circle. Cover the dough and let it rest for at least 30 minutes (or up to 2 hours) to allow the dough to relax and make it easier for the final roll.
5. Using a rolling pin, roll each paratha out into an 8-inch (20cm) diameter circle.

Cook and store the paratha (1 hour or 5 minutes per paratha)

1. Heat a cast-iron skillet or nonstick pan over medium-low heat. Add a small amount of butter to the skillet or pan before cooking each paratha.
2. Cook each paratha for 2 to 3 minutes on one side, then flip and cook for an additional 2 to 3 minutes until golden and flaky. Place the cooked paratha on a wire rack to cool. Repeat with the remaining paratha.
3. Store in an airtight container at room temperature for up to 2 days. If freezing, place a sheet of wax paper in between each paratha, transfer to a freezer bag, and freeze for up to 3 months. Reheat in a warm skillet.

CHAPTER 8

Sweet Sourdough Breads

Total time: 40 hours
Active prep time: 1 hour 10 minutes
Baking time: 55–65 minutes
Makes: 1 loaf

SPECIAL EQUIPMENT
Stand mixer fitted with a dough hook (optional)
One 8.5 × 4.75 × 4.375-inch (22 × 12 × 11cm) loaf pan

INGREDIENTS

Sweet stiff starter
50g unfed 100%-hydration sourdough starter
66g tap water
120g all-purpose flour
20g granulated sugar

Dough
105g tap water
105g any type of milk (I use 2%)
All of the sweet stiff starter
105g granulated sugar
2 medium eggs
8g fine sea salt
500g white bread flour
85g unsalted butter, softened

Chocolate spread
95g semisweet chocolate, melted
60g butter, melted
65g confectioners' sugar
18g cocoa powder

Simple syrup
120g water
100g granulated sugar

Fluffy Chocolate Babka

Indulge in the rich, fluffy goodness of this sourdough chocolate babka, where Jewish tradition meets natural leavening. This recipe uses a sweet stiff starter, which minimizes the sour profile sourdough is often known for. The dough is pillowy soft—enjoy it fresh from the oven or warm it up for breakfast the next day. Either way, this babka will become a beloved staple in your baking repertoire.

Prepare the sweet stiff starter (5 minutes active, 12-hour rise)

1. Prepare the sweet stiff starter the night before making the dough by mixing all starter ingredients together in a 1-liter (34fl oz) container. Cover the starter with plastic wrap and let it rise until it is at peak or has just started to fall (at least 12 hours).

Prepare the dough (40 minutes active, 3–10 hour bulk proof at room temperature, overnight cold proof)

1. The next morning, in a medium bowl or the bowl of a stand mixer, combine the water, milk, starter, sugar, eggs, salt, and flour. Mix on low for 10 minutes or knead by hand for 15 minutes until the ingredients are fully incorporated.
2. Gradually add the butter to the dough 1 to 2 tablespoons at a time, kneading until the butter is fully incorporated after each addition. Mix on low for 10 minutes after all the butter has been incorporated. (You may knead by hand for 15 minutes instead.) Cover the dough with a bowl cover or plastic wrap and let it rest.
3. *(Optional gluten development for a more shreddable crumb. If you wish to skip this step, proceed to step 4.)* Once 30 minutes have elapsed, perform a coil fold (p. 35). Perform two more coil folds in 30-minute intervals, covering the dough between each fold.
4. Cover the dough with a bowl cover or plastic wrap and let the dough proof until it has doubled in volume. (This may take 3 to 10 hours depending on the ambient room temperature.) Place the dough in the refrigerator for an overnight cold proof.

Make spread, shape, and final proof (15 minutes active, 2–8 hours final proof)

1. The next morning, prepare the loaf pan by coating it with butter or cooking spray.
2. Make the chocolate spread by combining all ingredients in a medium bowl and mixing with a whisk until smooth.
3. Lightly dust the work surface with flour. Use a rolling pin to roll the dough out to a 12 × 16-inch (30 × 41cm) rectangle. Using an offset spatula, spread the chocolate mixture evenly across the full surface of the dough. Roll up the dough from the short side to form a log. Cut the log in half lengthwise. With the cut sides facing up, twist the two halves around each other.
4. Place the dough in the prepared loaf pan, cover with a bowl cover or plastic wrap, and allow the dough to proof until puffy and finger-poke test produces a slow return of the dough. (This may take 2 to 8 hours depending on the ambient room temperature.)

Bake and store the babka (55–65 minutes)

1. Preheat the oven to 375°F (190°C).
2. Bake the dough for 55 to 65 minutes or until the internal temperature reaches 195°F (91°C).
3. While the babka is baking, prepare the simple syrup by bringing the water and sugar to a gentle boil in a small saucepot. Boil, stirring often, until the sugar has dissolved.
4. Once the babka has been removed from the oven, immediately brush or spoon the syrup over the entire top. Allow the babka to remain in the loaf pan for 15 minutes before removing and transferring to a rack to cool for another 45 minutes.
5. Store in an airtight container to maintain freshness for up to 3 days or slice the uncoated babka and freeze in a freezer bag for up to 2 months. This babka is best warmed in a microwave or an oven prior to eating.

Fluffy Poppyseed Babka

Total time: 40 hours
Active prep time: 1 hour 10 minutes
Baking time: 55–65 minutes
Makes: 1 loaf

SPECIAL EQUIPMENT

Stand mixer fitted with a dough hook (optional)
One 8.5 × 4.75 × 4.375-inch (22 × 12 × 11cm) loaf pan

INGREDIENTS

Sweet stiff starter

50g unfed 100%-hydration sourdough starter
66g tap water
120g all-purpose flour
20g granulated sugar

Dough

105g tap water
105g any type of milk (I use 2%)
All of the sweet stiff starter
105g granulated sugar
2 medium eggs
8g fine sea salt
500g white bread flour
85g unsalted butter, softened and divided

Poppyseed spread

120g ground poppy seeds
100g granulated sugar
53g flour
100g milk
Zest of one large orange or lemon (optional)
Pinch of salt

Citrus syrup

120g water
100g granulated sugar
Zest of 3 oranges or 3 lemons

This recipe is a tribute to the Rideau Bakery in Ottawa, where I first tasted a poppyseed roll that left a lasting impression. I can still recall the satisfying pop of the seeds between my teeth and the sweet filling wrapped in a soft, rich dough—it's one of my top Ottawa food memories. Though the bakery sadly closed its doors in 2019, I've recreated that beloved experience in my own kitchen ... with a twist (literally!). This babka is tender, decadent, and swirled with a fragrant and generous layer of poppyseed crunch.

Prepare the sweet stiff starter (5 minutes active, 12 hours rise)

1. Prepare the sweet stiff starter the night before making the dough by mixing all starter ingredients together in a 1-liter (34fl oz) container. Cover the starter with plastic wrap and let it rise until at peak or has just started to fall (at least 12 hours).

Prepare the dough (40 minutes active, 3–10 hours bulk proof at room temperature, overnight cold proof)

1. The next morning, combine the water, milk, starter, sugar, eggs, salt, and flour in a medium bowl or the bowl of a stand mixer. Mix on low for 10 minutes or knead by hand for 15 minutes until the ingredients are fully incorporated.
2. Gradually add the butter to the dough, 1 to 2 tablespoons at a time, and knead until the butter is fully incorporated after each addition. Mix on low for 10 minutes after all the butter has been incorporated. (You may knead by hand for 15 minutes instead.) Cover the dough with a bowl cover or plastic wrap and let it rest.
3. *(Optional step for gluten development for a more shreddable crumb. If you wish to skip this step, proceed to step 4.)* Once 30 minutes have elapsed, perform a coil fold (p. 35). Perform two more coil folds in 30-minute intervals, covering the dough between each fold.
4. Cover the dough with a bowl cover or plastic wrap and let the dough proof until it has doubled in volume. (This may take 3 to 10 hours depending on the ambient room temperature.) Place the dough in the refrigerator for an overnight cold proof.

Make spread, shape, and final proof (15 minutes active, 2–8 hours final proof)

1. The next morning, prepare the loaf pan by coating it with butter or cooking spray.
2. Make the poppyseed spread by whisking together poppyseeds, sugar, flour, milk, orange or lemon zest (if using), and salt in a small saucepot. Bring to a boil over medium heat, whisking continuously. When the mixture starts to thicken, switch to a wooden spoon or silicone spatula and stir until it is the consistency of a thick pudding.
3. Remove the spread from heat and transfer to a bowl to cool. Place it in the freezer to expedite cooling.
4. Remove the dough from the fridge. On a floured surface, use a rolling pin to roll the dough into a 12 × 16-inch (30 × 41cm) rectangle. Using an offset spatula, spread the poppyseed spread evenly across the full surface of the dough. Roll up the dough from the short side to form a log. Cut the log in half lengthwise. With the cut sides facing up, twist the two halves around each other.

5. Place the dough in the prepared loaf pan, cover with a bowl cover or plastic wrap, and allow the dough to proof until puffy and finger-poke test produces a slow return of the dough. (This may take 2 to 8 hours depending on the ambient room temperature.)

Bake and store the babka (55–65 minutes)

1. Preheat the oven to 375°F (190°C).
2. Bake the dough for 55 to 65 minutes or until the internal temperature reaches 195°F (91°C).
3. While the babka is baking, prepare the citrus syrup by bringing the water, sugar, and orange or lemon zest to a gentle boil in a small saucepot. Boil until the sugar has dissolved.
4. Once the babka has been removed from the oven, immediately brush or spoon the syrup over the entire top. Allow the babka to remain in the loaf pan for 15 minutes before removing it from the pan and transferring it to a rack to cool for another 45 minutes.
5. Store in an airtight container to maintain freshness for up to 3 days or slice the uncoated babka and freeze in a freezer bag for up to 2 months. This babka is best warmed in a microwave or an oven prior to eating.

Total time: 40 hours
Active prep time: 1 hour 10 minutes
Baking time: 55–65 minutes
Makes: 1 loaf

SPECIAL EQUIPMENT

Stand mixer fitted with a dough hook (optional)
One 8.5 × 4.75 × 4.375-inch (22 × 12 × 11cm) loaf pan

INGREDIENTS

Sweet stiff starter
50g unfed 100%-hydration sourdough starter
66g tap water
120g all-purpose flour
20g granulated sugar

Dough
105g tap water
105g any type of milk (I use 2%)
All of the sweet stiff starter
105g granulated sugar
2 medium eggs
8g fine sea salt
500g white bread flour
85g unsalted butter, softened

Cinnamon spread
150g unsalted butter, softened
16g ground cinnamon
120g light brown sugar
6 grams all-purpose flour

Simple syrup
120g water
100g granulated sugar

Fluffy Cinnamon Babka

This cinnamon babka is a pillow-soft loaf made with sweet stiff starter, which mutes the sourness that sourdough is most known for. With each bite, you'll enjoy the flavors and texture of fluffy, enriched dough and warm, aromatic cinnamon filling. It's the perfect loaf for those who love a sweet, enriched bread and want to enjoy the benefits of leavening with sourdough.

Prepare the sweet stiff starter (5 minutes active, 12 hours rise)

1. Prepare the sweet stiff starter the night before making the dough by mixing all starter ingredients together in a 1-liter (34fl oz) container. Cover the starter with plastic wrap and let it rise until at peak or has just started to fall, at least 12 hours.

Prepare the dough (40 minutes active, 3–10 hours bulk proof at room temperature, overnight cold proof)

1. The next morning, in a medium bowl or the bowl of a stand mixer, combine the water, milk, starter, sugar, eggs, salt, and flour. Mix on low for 10 minutes or knead by hand for 15 minutes until the ingredients are fully incorporated.
2. Gradually add the butter to the dough 1 to 2 tablespoons at a time, kneading until the butter is fully incorporated after each addition. Mix on low for 10 minutes after all the butter has been incorporated. (You may knead by hand for 15 minutes instead.) Cover the dough with a bowl cover or plastic wrap and let it rest.
3. *(Optional step for gluten development for a more shreddable crumb. If you wish to skip this step, proceed to step 4.)* Once 30 minutes have elapsed, perform a coil fold (p. 35). Perform two more coil folds in 30-minute intervals, covering the dough between each fold.
4. Cover the dough with a bowl cover or plastic wrap and let the dough proof until it has doubled in volume. (This may take 3 to 10 hours depending on the ambient room temperature.) Place the dough in the refrigerator for an overnight cold proof.

Make the spread, shape and final proof (15 minutes active, 2–8 hours final proof)

1. The next morning, prepare the loaf pan by coating it with butter or cooking spray.
2. Make the cinnamon spread by combining all ingredients and mixing them together with a wooden spoon until smooth.
3. Lightly dust the work surface with flour. Use a rolling pin to roll the dough out to a 12 × 16-inch (30 × 41cm) rectangle. Using an offset spatula, spread the cinnamon spread evenly across the full surface of the dough. Roll up the dough from the short side to form a log. Cut the log in half lengthwise. With the cut sides facing up, twist the two halves around each other.
4. Place the dough in the prepared loaf pan, cover with a bowl cover or plastic wrap, and allow the dough to proof until puffy and finger-poke test produces a slow return of the dough. (This may take 2 to 8 hours depending on the ambient room temperature.)

Bake and store the babka (55–65 minutes)

1. Preheat the oven to 375°F (190°C).
2. Bake the dough for 55 to 65 minutes or until the internal temperature reaches 195°F (91°C).
3. While the babka is baking, prepare the simple syrup by bringing the water and sugar to a gentle boil in a small saucepot. Boil, stirring often, until the sugar has dissolved.
4. Once the babka has been removed from the oven, immediately brush or spoon the syrup over the entire top. Allow the babka to remain in the loaf pan for 15 minutes before removing it from the pan and transferring it to a rack to cool for another 45 minutes.
5. Store in an airtight container to maintain freshness for up to 3 days or slice the uncoated babka and freeze in a freezer bag for up to 2 months. This babka is best warmed in a microwave or an oven prior to eating.

Total time: 36 hours
Active prep time: 1 hour 15 minutes
Baking time: 45–60 minutes
Makes: One wool-roll loaf

SPECIAL EQUIPMENT

Stand mixer fitted with a dough hook (optional)
One 8-inch (20.5cm) diameter by 3-inch (7.5cm) tall cake tin or bundt pan

INGREDIENTS

Dough

75g any type of milk (I use 2%)
190g active 100%-hydration sourdough starter
50g granulated sugar
3 medium eggs, divided
7g fine sea salt
370g strong white bread flour
120g unsalted butter (softened)

Apple butter

1,020g peeled and cubed Granny Smith apples (about 5–6)
150g granulated sugar
90g light brown sugar
1g salt
3g ground cinnamon
1g grated nutmeg
7g apple cider vinegar

Candied walnuts

75g chopped walnut pieces
38g light brown sugar
10g unsalted butter

Apple Butter and Candied Walnut Wool Roll

Why not treat yourself to this shreddable, fluffy autumn treat that is beautifully shaped into a wool roll and packed with warm spice? This sourdough-leavened bread is filled with homemade apple butter and crunchy, caramelized walnuts, making every bite a balance of tart, sweet, and earthy flavors. This bread is a showstopper with a gorgeous swirl, so be sure to share it with friends and family.

Make and proof the dough (40 minutes active, 4–10 hours bulk proof at room temperature, overnight cold proof)

1. In a medium bowl or the bowl of a stand mixer, combine the milk, starter, sugar, 2 eggs, salt, and flour. Knead on low for 10 minutes. Alternatively, you can knead by hand for 15 minutes.
2. Gradually add the butter to the dough, 1 to 2 tablespoons at a time, kneading until the butter is fully incorporated after each addition. Knead by hand or in the stand mixer for 20 to 30 minutes until the dough is smooth and elastic.
3. Cover the dough with a bowl cover or plastic wrap and let the dough bulk proof until it has doubled in volume. (This may take 4 to 10 hours depending on the ambient room temperature.) Place the covered bowl in the refrigerator for an overnight cold proof.

Make the apple butter and candied walnuts (15 minutes active)

1. While the dough is proofing, make the apple butter by combining all ingredients in a medium saucepan. Cook uncovered over medium heat until bubbling, then reduce the heat to medium low and cook for 2 hours, stirring occasionally with a rubber spatula. After 2 hours reduce the heat to low. Cook for 2 hours more, stirring occasionally. (The apple butter should be thick and a deep brown color.) Transfer the apple butter to a bowl, cover, and refrigerate until dough shaping.
2. Make the candied walnuts by adding all the ingredients to nonstick pan placed over medium heat. Stirring constantly, heat until the sugar is bubbling, ensuring the sugar is melted and the nuts are fully coated in the melted sugar, about 3 to 5 minutes. Remove the pan from the heat and transfer the walnuts to a sheet of parchment paper to cool. Once cool, transfer the walnuts to a covered bowl until dough shaping.

Shape and final proof (20 minutes active, 3–8 hours final proof)

1. The next morning, prepare the cake tin or bundt pan by coating it with butter or cooking spray.
2. Remove the dough from the fridge and cut into five 181-gram balls. Roll one ball into a 4 × 8-inch (10 × 20cm) rectangle (rounded corners are fine). Using a bench scraper, cut thin strips of dough lengthwise along the top half of the rectangle. Spread ⅕ of the apple butter on the bottom half of the dough and sprinkle with ⅕ of the walnuts. Repeat the process for the remaining 4 balls.
3. Whisk the remaining egg in a small bowl to create the egg wash. Roll the dough, starting from the bottom (short side) to form a log. Line the perimeter of the pan with the five logs. (You may have to squeeze them in.) Brush the dough with the egg wash. Cover and let the dough rise until airy and jiggly, and a finger poke produces a slow return of the dough. (This may take 3 to 8 hours depending on the ambient room temperature.)

Bake and store the roll (45–60 minutes)

1. Preheat the oven to 350°F (175°C).
2. Coat the dough again in egg wash. Bake the dough for 45 to 60 minutes or until the internal temperature reaches 195°F (91°C). Remove the roll from the cake tin or bundt pan and let it cool on a wire rack for 1 hour before slicing.
3. Store the roll at room temperature in an airtight container or resealable bag for up to 3 days or freeze, sliced, in a freezer bag for up to 2 months.

Total time: 36 hours
Active prep time: 45 minutes
Baking time: 20–25 minutes
Makes: 12 buns

SPECIAL EQUIPMENT

Stand mixer fitted with a dough hook (optional)
Piping bag

INGREDIENTS

Dough

52g tap water
52g any type of milk (I use 2%)
100g active 100%-hydration sourdough starter
50g granulated sugar
2 medium eggs, divided
4g sea salt
220g white bread flour
42g unsalted butter, softened and divided

Filling and topping

230g Nutella
Confectioners' sugar (optional)

Nutella-Filled Buns

These pillowy sourdough buns are filled with rich, creamy Nutella and baked to golden perfection. Soft, buttery, and just the right amount of indulgent, they are perfect for an afternoon tea sweet or an after-dinner dessert. One bite and you'll be hooked!

Make and proof the dough (30 minutes active, 3–10 hours bulk proof at room temperature, overnight cold proof)

1. Add the water, milk, starter, sugar, 1 egg, salt, and flour to a medium bowl or to the bowl of a stand mixer. Mix on low for 10 minutes or knead by hand for 15 minutes until fully incorporated.
2. Slowly add the butter to the dough, 1 to 2 tablespoons at a time, and mix until the butter is fully incorporated each time. Mix on low for 20 minutes after all the butter has been incorporated, or knead by hand for 30 minutes.
3. Cover the dough with a bowl cover or plastic wrap and let the dough proof until doubled in size. (This may take 3 to 10 hours depending on the ambient room temperature.) Place the dough in the refrigerator for an overnight cold proof.

Shape and final proof (15 minutes active, 2–8 hours final proof)

1. The next morning, prepare a baking sheet by lining it with parchment paper.
2. Remove the dough from the refrigerator and, using a bench scraper or sharp knife, divide it into twelve equal-size pieces (45g to 50g each). Shape the pieces into balls and then place each ball on the parchment-lined baking sheet.
3. Cover the dough balls loosely with plastic wrap and allow the dough to proof until it has doubled in size, is puffy, and a finger-poke test produces a slow return of the dough. (This may take 2 to 8 hours depending on the ambient room temperature.)

Bake, top, and store the buns (15–20 minutes)

1. Preheat the oven to 375°F (190°C).
2. Whisk the remaining egg in a small bowl. Brush the buns with the egg wash.
3. Bake the buns for 15 to 20 minutes or until the internal temperature reaches 195°F (91°C). Cool the buns on a wire rack.
4. Fill a piping bag with the Nutella and snip the tip of the piping bag.
5. Once the buns have cooled, use a chopstick or skewer to make a hole in the center of each bun. Place the tip of piping bag into the hole until you reach resistance. Squeeze a generous amount of Nutella into the bun, then dust the tops with confectioners' sugar.
6. Store the buns in an airtight container to maintain freshness for up to 2 days or freeze unfilled and undusted buns in a freezer bag for up to 2 months.

Total time: 40 hours
Active prep time: 1 hour 35 minutes
Baking time: 15–30 minutes (2–4 minutes per donut)
Makes: 20 donuts

SPECIAL EQUIPMENT

Stand mixer fitted with a dough hook (optional)
Oil thermometer (optional)
Slotted spoon or stainless-steel spider strainer
Stainless steel tongs
Piping bag

INGREDIENTS

Dough

105g tap water
105g any type of milk (I use 2%)
200g 100%-hydration active sourdough starter
105g granulated sugar
2 medium eggs
7g sea salt
540g white bread flour
2g ground nutmeg
85g unsalted butter, divided
950–1,200g vegetable oil, for frying (the oil should be 2 inches [5cm] deep in the pot)

Filling

460g plum jam (or filling of your choice)

Glaze

140g confectioners' sugar
20–25g any type of milk (I use 2%)
Pinch of salt
Zest from 1 orange

Plum-Filled Donuts (Polish Pączki)

I have such fond memories of visiting a local European bakery with my Polish nanny. She would treat my sister and me to plum jam-filled *pączki*—pillowy, golden donuts, shiny with a sweet glaze and bursting with jammy plum goodness. These fluffy, naturally leavened filled donuts take me right back to that joyful time. Whether for breakfast or dessert, these donuts are an irresistible indulgence.

Make and proof the dough (30 minutes active, 3–10 hours bulk proof at room temperature, overnight cold proof)

1. Add the water, milk, starter, sugar, eggs, salt, flour, and nutmeg to a medium bowl or to the bowl of a stand mixer. Mix on low for 10 minutes or knead by hand for 15 minutes until fully incorporated.
2. Slowly add the butter to the dough, 1 to 2 tablespoons at a time, and mix until the butter is fully incorporated each time. Mix on low for 20 minutes after all the butter has been incorporated, or knead by hand for 30 minutes.
3. Cover the dough with a bowl cover or plastic wrap and let the dough proof until doubled in size. (This may take 3 to 10 hours depending on the ambient room temperature.) Place the dough in the refrigerator for an overnight cold proof.

Shape and final proof (15 minutes active, 2–8 hours final proof)

1. The next morning, prepare twenty parchment paper squares, 2.5 inches (6.5cm) each, and place them on a large baking sheet.
2. Remove the dough from the fridge and, using a bench scraper or sharp knife, divide it into twenty 60g pieces. Shape the pieces into balls and then place each ball on a parchment square on the baking sheet.
3. Cover the dough balls loosely with plastic wrap and allow the dough to proof until doubled in size, puffy, and a finger-poke test produces a slow return of the dough. (This may take 2 to 8 hours depending on the ambient room temperature.)

Fry the donuts (1 hour active)

1. Pour 2 inches (5cm) of oil into a large, heavy-bottomed pot placed over medium heat. Heat the oil until it reaches 350°F (177°C) on an oil thermometer. (I have used a meat thermometer to measure the temperature of the oil; however, for consistent results, using an oil thermometer attached to the side of the pot will work best.)
2. Pick a donut up by the parchment square's corners and carefully place it topside down into the hot oil. Add three to four donuts to the pot at a time. After 1 to 2 minutes, turn the donuts to the parchment-lined side with the slotted spoon or spider strainer and, with stainless steel tongs, remove the parchment paper pieces from the oil. Cook the donuts for additional 1 to 2 minutes, then carefully transfer a donut with the slotted spoon or spider strainer to a paper—towel lined plate or tray. Repeat with remaining donuts. (Note: If you are not using an oil thermometer, I recommend checking the temperature of the oil after each batch to ensure it is staying within the range of 340°F to 350°F [171°C to 177°C].)

Fill, glaze, and store the donuts (10 minutes active)

1. Prepare the glaze by mixing all glaze ingredients in a small bowl.
2. Prepare the plum jam by stirring it to make it a smoother texture, then pour it into a piping bag. Snip the tip of the piping bag.
3. Once the donuts have cooled, use a chopstick or skewer to make a hole into the center of the donut. Place the piping bag into the donut until you feel resistance. Squeeze a generous amount into the donut, then dip the donut into the glaze.
4. Store the donuts in an airtight container to maintain freshness for up to 2 days or freeze the unfilled and unglazed donuts in a freezer bag for up to 2 months.

Total time: 33 hours
Active prep time: 90 minutes
Baking time: 45 minutes
Makes: 12 cinnamon buns

SPECIAL EQUIPMENT
Stand mixer fitted with a dough hook (optional)
One 9 × 13-inch (23 × 33cm) baking pan

INGREDIENTS

Sweet stiff starter
50g unfed 100%-hydration sourdough starter
66g tap water
120g all-purpose flour
20g granulated sugar

Tangzhong
120g any type of milk (I use 2%)
23g all-purpose flour

Dough
130g tap water
All of the sweet, stiff starter
All of the tangzhong
50g granulated sugar
50g neutral oil (I use avocado oil)
5g sea salt
400g white bread flour

Cinnamon-sugar filling
125g granulated sugar
25g ground cinnamon
75g unsalted butter, softened and divided

Topping
120g heavy whipping cream

Icing
120g confectioner's sugar
15g any type of milk (I use 2%)
4g vanilla extract
Pinch of salt

Fluffy Overnight Cinnamon Buns

These pillowy buns are a decadent treat and are swirled with delicious cinnamon goodness. Made with a tangzhong and a sweet stiff starter, their soft crumb is unmatched. Topped with heavy whipping cream right before baking, these slow-fermented cinnamon buns become a gooey, finger-licking treat you will want to make again and again.

Prepare the sweet stiff starter (5 minutes active, 12 hours rise)

1. Prepare the sweet stiff starter in the morning by mixing all starter ingredients together in a 1-liter (34fl oz) container. Cover the starter with plastic wrap and let it rise until at peak or has just started to fall (at least 12 hours).

Make the tanzhong and the dough (40 minutes active, overnight bulk proof at room temperature)

1. In the evening of the same day, make the tangzhong by whisking together the milk and flour in a small saucepan. Cook over medium heat, stirring constantly, until thickened to a pudding-like consistency. Remove from the heat and let cool to room temperature.
2. Make the dough that night by combining all dough ingredients in the bowl of a stand mixer or a medium bowl. Knead on low for 20 minutes or for 30 minutes by hand until the dough is soft and elastic. Cover and let proof at room temperature overnight.

Shape the buns and proof (15–20 minutes active, 2–8 hours final proof at room temperature)

1. The next morning, mix together the ingredients for the cinnamon-sugar filling to form a paste.
2. Gently deflate the dough. Roll it out on a floured surface and into a 15 × 18-inch (38 × 46cm) rectangle.
3. Spread the filling onto the entire surface of the dough and roll it up (not too tightly) from the long side.
4. Lightly mark the dough at 1.5-inch (4cm) intervals to make twelve rolls.
5. Cut the dough at the demarcations with a serrated knife or sewing thread.
6. Prepare the baking pan by greasing it with butter or cooking spray. Place the cinnamon buns into the pan. Cover with plastic wrap or a damp towel and allow the dough to proof until it has doubled in volume, is puffy, and a finger-poke test produces a slow return of the dough. (This may take 2 to 8 hours depending on the ambient room temperature.)

Bake and store the buns (45 minutes)

1. Preheat the oven to 325°F (165°C).
2. Pour the heavy whipping cream evenly over the buns.
3. Bake for 45 minutes or until deeply golden and the internal temperature reaches 195°F (91°C). If they brown too quickly, loosely tent with foil halfway through baking.
4. Let the buns cool on a wire rack in the pan for 15 to 20 minutes.
5. While the buns are cooling, whisk together the confectioner's sugar, milk, vanilla, and salt in a small bowl until smooth and pourable. Drizzle the icing over the still-warm buns.
6. These are best served the day of baking, but can be kept in an airtight container at room temperature for up to 3 days or frozen in a freezer bag for up to 2 months.

Cardamom Knots

Total time: 36 hours
Active prep time: 1 hour 5 minutes
Baking time: 20–25 minutes
Makes: 24 knots

SPECIAL EQUIPMENT

Stand mixer fitted with a dough hook (optional)

INGREDIENTS

Sweet stiff starter

50g 100%-hydration sourdough starter
66g tap water
120g all-purpose flour
20g granulated sugar

Dough

45g tap water
45g any type of milk (I use 2%)
All of the sweet stiff starter
50g granulated sugar
1 medium egg
4g sea salt
250g white bread flour
40g unsalted butter, softened

Cardamom paste

2g ground cinnamon
4g ground cardamom
65g light brown sugar
50g unsalted butter, softened

Cardamom glaze (optional)

230g confectioners' sugar
46g any type of milk (I use 2%)
3g vanilla extract
2g ground cardamom
Pinch of salt

Featuring a blend of warm spices and leavened with sweet stiff starter, these cardamom knots have a golden, crispy crust and soft interior. The sweet stiff starter softens the tang of the sourdough, so in spite of the long fermentation, these will not have your typical sour profile. These knots are best enjoyed fresh out of the oven!

Prepare the sweet stiff starter (5 minutes active, 12 hours rise)

1. Prepare the sweet stiff starter in the morning by mixing all starter ingredients together in a 1-liter (34fl oz) container. Cover the starter with plastic wrap and let it rise until at peak or has just started to fall (at least 12 hours).

Make the dough (50 minutes active, bulk proof at room temperature for 2–8 hours, overnight cold proof)

1. The next morning, in a medium bowl or the bowl of a stand mixer, combine the water, milk, starter, sugar, egg, salt, and flour. Mix on low for 10 minutes. Alternatively, you can knead by hand for 15 minutes or until the ingredients are fully incorporated.
2. Gradually add the butter to the dough, 1 to 2 tablespoons at a time, and knead until it is fully incorporated after each addition. Knead by hand or in the stand mixer for 20 to 30 minutes until the dough is smooth and elastic. Cover the dough with a bowl cover or plastic wrap and let it rest for 1 hour.
3. *(Optional step for gluten development for a more shreddable crumb. If you wish to skip this step, proceed to step 4.)* Once 1 hour has elapsed, perform a coil fold (p. 35). Perform two more coil folds in 30-minute intervals, covering the dough between each fold. Cover and let the dough proof until it has doubled in volume. (This may take 2 to 8 hours depending on the ambient room temperature.) Place the covered dough in the refrigerator for an overnight cold proof.
4. Cover and let the dough proof until it has doubled in volume. (This may take 2 to 8 hours depending on the ambient room temperature.) Place the covered dough in the refrigerator for an overnight cold proof.

Shape and final proof (30 minutes active, 2–8 hours final proof)

1. The next morning, mix all the ingredients for the cardamom paste in a small bowl until fully blended.
2. Line a cookie sheet with parchment paper, and lightly dust the work surface with flour. Using a rolling pin, roll the dough into a 12 × 24-inch (30 × 61cm) rectangle. Spread the cardamom paste evenly over the full expanse of the dough. Fold the dough into thirds on the short side. On the long side, mark the dough at 1-inch (2.5cm) intervals.
3. Cut the dough into twenty-four 1-inch (2.5cm) strips. Cut each strip into thirds, leaving one side joined. Braid the strips to create a three-stranded plait. Roll up the plait from the joined side and place the knots on the cookie sheet. Cover the knots with plastic wrap and a cotton towel and proof until knots are doubled in size, puffy, and a finger-poke produces a slow return of the dough. (This may take 2 to 8 hours, depending on the ambient room temperature.)

Bake, glaze, and store the knots (20–25 minutes)

1. Preheat the oven to 375°F (190°C).
2. Prepare the cardamom glaze by mixing all ingredients in a small bowl until no lumps remain.

3. Bake the knots for 20 to 25 minutes or until the internal temperature reaches 195°F (91°C). Brush the cardamom glaze over the still-warm knots. Enjoy the knots warm and fresh out of the oven.
4. Store in an airtight container to maintain freshness for up to 5 days or freeze in a freezer bag for up to 2 months. These are best warmed in the microwave or an oven prior to eating.

Total time: 36–40 hours
Active prep time: 1 hour 15 minutes
Baking time: 20–25 minutes
Makes: 8 croissants

SPECIAL EQUIPMENT

Stand mixer fitted with a dough hook (optional)
Laser thermometer (optional)

INGREDIENTS

Dough

105g tap water
100g any type of milk (I use 2%)
270g active 100%-hydration sourdough starter
70g granulated sugar
40g neutral oil (I use avocado oil)
8g fine sea salt
450g all-purpose flour
1 medium egg (for egg wash)

Beurrage (butter block)

240g unsalted butter, room temperature

Buttery Croissants

For years, croissants were my baking nemesis. No matter how carefully I followed techniques for keeping butter pliable, it would crack and tear through my dough, leaving me frustrated and defeated. The breakthrough came when I realized my struggle wasn't with technique—it was with the ingredients. In Canada, finding butter with high milk-fat content (above 82 percent) can be incredibly challenging. Most supermarket butters simply don't have the fat content needed for proper lamination. Once I invested in high-quality European butter and discovered that the ideal rolling temperature is around 63°F (17°C), everything changed. Suddenly, my croissants transformed from disasters into golden, flaky masterpieces.

The process for making these croissants is undeniably long, but there's something deeply satisfying about rolling out each layer by hand, knowing you're creating something extraordinary through patience and care. I've learned that slightly underkneading the dough makes it easier to handle, as the lamination process develops the gluten further. These croissants are definitely a weekend project, but the reward is unmatched.

Prepare the dough (5–8 minutes, 4–8 hours proof, 1 hour chill)

1. In a medium bowl or the bowl of a stand mixer, combine the water, milk, starter, sugar, oil, salt, and flour. Mix on low for 5 to 8 minutes or just until a soft dough forms. Alternatively, knead by hand for 10 to 12 minutes. (Knead only lightly, as the rolling and folding will further develop the gluten.)
2. Cover the dough with a bowl cover or plastic wrap and let it proof at room temperature until it has doubled in size. (This can take from 4 to 8 hours depending on the ambient room temperature.) Once the dough has risen accordingly, transfer it to the refrigerator and chill for 1 hour to make it easier to roll and laminate.

Make the beurrage and laminate the dough (45 minutes active, two 45-minute resting rounds)

1. While the dough is chilling, cut a piece of parchment paper that measures at least 13 × 17 inches (33 × 43cm). Using a pencil and a ruler, draw a 6.5 × 8.5-inch (16.5 × 22cm) rectangle in the center of the parchment paper. Flip the paper over so the pencil markings are on the underside of the parchment paper and then fold the paper where the pencil markings appear to make a visible crease. Unfold the parchment paper. (The pencil markings will not touch the butter.)
2. Spread the room-temperature butter out evenly across the parchment paper within the lines of the penciled rectangle. (I use an offset spatula to easily spread the butter.) Fold the parchment paper over the butter so it is completely encased within the demarcated lines, using the creases to encase the butter. Use a rolling pin to gently roll the butter evenly to the corners of the parchment paper. This is your beurrage.
3. Once 1 hour has elapsed, remove the dough from the refrigerator and place the beurrage in the refrigerator. Dust your work surface generously with flour, and roll the dough out to a 9 × 13-inch (23 × 33cm) rectangle.
4. Using a laser thermometer, if you have one, check that the beurrage is between 63°F and 66°F (17°C and 19°C) and the dough is around the same temperature. If the dough is cooler, leave it rolled out on the work surface and place the beurrage back in the refrigerator. If the beurrage is colder, use a rolling pin to hammer it slightly and run your hands along the surface of the paper to quickly

warm it. If you do not have a laser thermometer, compare with touch to determine if both are similar in temperature; you want both to feel slightly cool to touch but not cold. It is also important to ensure your butter is pliable before folding it in. Bend it and if it bends without breaking, it is pliable enough to be folded in. When both the beurrage and the dough are at the proper temperature, place the beurrage in the center of the dough so the long side of the butter aligns with the short side of the dough. Remove the parchment paper. Fold the long sides of the dough to meet in the middle and over the beurrage, and pinch it down the middle to seal the butter in the dough.

5. Tap the dough with a rolling pin to help lock the butter into the dough. With gentle pressure, roll it out into a neat 8 × 18-inch (20 x 46cm) rectangle with the short side facing you.
6. Fold the short side facing you about 3 inches (8cm) toward the middle of the dough. Fold the opposite short side to meet it so they align. Pinch the ends together. Fold the entire dough in half again on the short side. You have just made a double fold. Wrap the dough in plastic wrap and refrigerate for 30 minutes, then remove it from the refrigerator and allow it to rest at room temperature for 15 minutes.
7. Once the resting time has elapsed, with gentle pressure, roll the dough out to about 8 × 15 inches (20 × 38cm). Fold the dough in thirds like a letter: Start by folding a short side in about 5 inches (13cm) toward the middle of the dough, then take the other edge and fold it over the already folded portion. Wrap the dough in plastic wrap and refrigerate for another 30 minutes. Remove it from the refrigerator and allow it to rest at room temperature for 15 minutes.

Shape and final proof (20 minutes active, overnight cold proof, 2–6 hours final proof)

1. Roll the dough out to approximately 9 × 20 inches (23 × 51cm). Trim the edges for clean lines. Cut the dough into eight even triangles and then roll each one up from the base to the tip to shape the croissants.
2. Place the shaped croissants spaced evenly on a parchment-lined baking sheet. Cover completely with plastic wrap and a tea towel and refrigerate overnight.
3. The next morning, bring the croissants to room temperature and let them proof until puffy and jiggly and a finger-poke test reveals a slow return of the dough. (This may take 2 to 6 hours depending on the ambient room temperature.)

Bake and store the croissants (20–25 minutes active)

1. Preheat the oven to 400°F (205°C).
2. Whisk the egg in a small bowl. Brush each croissant with the egg wash, avoiding the visible lamination to prevent sticking.
3. Bake for 20 to 25 minutes or until deep golden and crisp and the internal temperature measures 200°F (93°C).
4. Cool on a wire rack for at least 30 minutes before eating.
5. Store the croissants in an airtight container at room temperature for up to 2 days or freeze in a freezer bag for up to 2 months. Reheat in a 325°F (165°C) oven for 5 to 8 minutes.

Total time: 14–38 hours
Active prep time: 1 hour 15 minutes
Baking time: 18–22 minutes
Makes: 20 pain aux raisins

SPECIAL EQUIPMENT

Stand mixer fitted with a dough hook (optional)
Laser thermometer (optional)

INGREDIENTS

Dough

105g tap water
100g any type of milk (I use 2%)
270g 100%-hydration active sourdough starter
70g granulated sugar
40g neutral oil (I use avocado oil)
8g fine sea salt
415g all-purpose flour
1 medium egg (for egg wash)

Beurrage (butter block)

190g room-temperature unsalted butter

Custard

245g milk (I use 2%)
21g cornstarch
60g fine granulated sugar
4 medium egg yolks
Pinch of salt
7g unsalted butter
5g vanilla extract

Filling

120g freshly squeezed orange juice
120g raisins (any type)

Glaze

100g confectioners' sugar
15–20g freshly squeezed orange juice or milk
Zest of 1 orange

Sprinkling

Pearl sugar (optional)

Pain aux Raisins

These elegant, spiraled pastries are filled with custard and dotted with orange-soaked raisins. They make an excellent breakfast with a warm cup of tea, or can be enjoyed as a sweet afternoon indulgence. The flavor is brightened by the orange-soaked raisins and zesty glaze, while the sourdough offers a subtle depth of flavor. These are definitely a weekend project. And while you *can* make them in a single day, I recommend extending the process over two days.

Make the dough (12 minutes active, 4–8 hours bulk proof at room temperature, 1 hour cold proof)

1. In a medium bowl or the bowl of a stand mixer, combine the water, milk, starter, sugar, oil, salt, and flour. Mix on low for 5 to 8 minutes or just until a soft dough forms. Alternatively, knead by hand for 10 to 12 minutes. (Knead only lightly, as the rolling and folding will further develop gluten.)
2. Cover the dough with a bowl cover or plastic wrap and let proof at room temperature until doubled in size. (This can take from 4 to 8 hours depending on the ambient room temperature.) Once the dough has risen accordingly, transfer it to the refrigerator and chill for 1 hour to make it easier to roll and laminate.

Make the beurrage and laminate the dough (45 minutes active, two 45-minute resting rounds)

1. While the dough is chilling, cut out a piece of parchment paper that measures at least 13 × 17 inches (33 × 43cm). Using a pencil and a ruler, draw a 6.5 × 8.5-inch (16.5 × 22cm) rectangle in the center of the parchment paper. Flip the paper over so the pencil markings are on the underside of the parchment paper and then fold the paper where the pencil markings appear to make a visible crease. Unfold the parchment paper. (The pencil markings will not touch the butter.)
2. Spread the room-temperature butter evenly across the parchment paper within the lines of the penciled rectangle. (I use an offset spatula to easily spread the butter.) Fold the parchment paper over the butter so it is completely encased within the demarcated lines, using the creases to encase the butter. Use a rolling pin to gently roll the butter evenly to the corners of the parchment paper. This is your beurrage.
3. Once 1 hour has elapsed, remove the dough from the refrigerator and place your beurrage in the refrigerator. Dust the work surface generously with flour and roll the dough out to a 9 × 13-inch (23 × 33cm) rectangle.
4. Using a laser thermometer, if you have one, check that the beurrage is between 63°F and 66°F (17°C and 19°C). Check the dough to ensure it is around the same temperature. If the dough is cooler, leave it rolled out on the work surface and place the beurrage back in the refrigerator. If the beurrage is colder, use a rolling pin to hammer it slightly and run your hands along the surface of the paper to quickly warm it. If you do not have a laser thermometer, compare with touch to determine if both are similar in temperature; you want both to feel slightly cool to touch but not cold. It is also important to ensure your butter is pliable before folding it in. Bend it and if it bends without breaking, it is pliable enough to be folded in. When both the beurrage and the dough are at the proper temperature, place the beurrage in the center of the dough so the long side of the butter aligns with the short side of the dough. Remove the parchment paper. Fold the long sides of the dough to meet in the middle, over the beurrage, and pinch it down the middle to seal in the butter.

5. Tap the dough with a rolling pin to help lock the butter into the dough. With gentle pressure, roll it out into a neat 8 × 18-inch (20 x 46cm) rectangle with the short side facing you.
6. Fold the short side facing you about 3 inches (8cm) toward the middle of the dough, then fold the opposite short side to meet it so the ends align. Pinch the ends together. Fold the entire dough in half again on the short side. You have just made a double fold. Wrap the dough in plastic wrap and refrigerate for 30 minutes, then remove it from the refrigerator and allow it to rest at room temperature for 15 minutes.
7. Once the resting time has elapsed, with gentle pressure, roll the dough out to about a 8 × 15-inch (20 × 38cm) rectangle. Fold the dough in thirds like a letter. start by folding a short side in about 5 inches (13cm) toward the middle of the dough, then take the other edge and fold it over the already folded portion. Wrap the dough in plastic wrap and refrigerate for another 30 minutes, then remove it from the refrigerator and allow it to rest at room temperature for 15 minutes.

Make the filling and the custard (20 minutes active, 30-minute cooldown)

1. In a medium, shallow bowl, mix together the orange juice and the raisins. Let the raisins sit for 15 to 20 minutes, then drain off any remaining juice and pat the raisins dry with a paper towel. Set aside.
2. In a small bowl, mix together the milk and cornstarch.
3. In a medium, heavy-bottomed pot, whisk together the milk mixture, sugar, egg yolks, and salt. Bring to a simmer over medium heat, whisking continuously. Cook for 2 to 3 minutes or until the custard is a pudding-like consistency. Remove from the heat and stir in the butter and vanilla.
4. Spread the custard over a large plate and cover with plastic wrap to prevent a skin from forming. Place the custard in the refrigerator for 30 minutes or the freezer for 15 minutes to help cool it down.

Shape and final proof (20 minutes active, 30 minutes to 24 hours refrigeration, 2–6 hours final proof)

1. Roll the dough out to approximately 9 × 20 inches (23 × 51cm). Trim the edges for clean lines.
2. Spread the cooled custard evenly over the dough and then sprinkle the raisins evenly over the top.
3. Roll the dough up from the long side, wrap in plastic wrap and refrigerate for 30 minutes up to 24 hours.
4. Remove the dough from the refrigerator and slice at 1-inch (2.5cm) intervals. Place the pieces on two parchment paper-lined baking sheets 2 inches (5cm) apart. Cover completely with plastic wrap and let them proof until puffy and the dough slowly springs back when gently poked. (This may take 2 to 6 hours depending on the duration of the cold ferment and the ambient room temperature.)

Bake, glaze, and store the pain aux raisins (18–22 minutes)

1. Preheat the oven to 375°F (190°C).
2. Sprinkle with pearl sugar (if using). Bake for 18 to 22 minutes or until deep golden and crisp. Transfer to a wire rack to cool.
3. While the pain aux raisins are cooling, whisk together the glaze ingredients and drizzle over the still-warm buns.
4. Store the pain aux raisins in an airtight container at room temperature for up to 2 days or freeze (unglazed) for up to 1 month. Reheat in a 325°F (165°C) oven for 5 to 8 minutes for best results.

Total time: 40 hours
Active prep time: 1 hour 5 minutes
Baking time: 20–25 minutes
Makes: 12 buns

SPECIAL EQUIPMENT

Stand mixer fitted with a dough hook (optional)

INGREDIENTS

Sweet, stiff starter

50g 100%-hydration sourdough starter
66g tap water
120g all-purpose flour
20g granulated sugar

Dough

65g tap water
65g any type of milk (I use 2%)
All of the sweet stiff starter
60g granulated sugar
2 medium eggs, divided
100g pumpkin purée
5g sea salt
400g all-purpose flour
3g ground cinnamon
40g unsalted butter, softened

Filling

24 dark chocolate sticks

Pumpkin Chocolate Buns

These soft autumn-inspired buns are flavored with pumpkin and a hint of cinnamon, and they feature a surprise dark chocolate stick inside! Using a sweet stiff sourdough starter, these buns are both light and naturally leavened.

Prepare the sweet stiff starter (5 minutes active, 12 hours rise)

1. Prepare the sweet stiff starter the night before making the dough by mixing all the starter ingredients together in a 1-liter (34fl oz) container. Cover the starter with plastic wrap and let it rise until at peak or has just started to fall, at least 12 hours.

Prepare the dough (40 minutes active, 3–10 hours bulk proof at room temperature, overnight cold proof)

1. The next morning, in a medium bowl or the bowl of a stand mixer, combine the water, milk, starter, sugar, 1 egg, pumpkin, salt, flour, and cinnamon. Mix on low for 10 minutes or knead by hand for 15 minutes until the ingredients are fully incorporated.
2. Gradually add the softened butter 1 to 2 tablespoons at a time, kneading until the butter is incorporated after each addition. Mix on low for 20 minutes after all the butter has been incorporated. (You may knead by hand for 30 minutes instead.)
3. Cover the dough with a bowl cover or plastic wrap and let it proof at room temperature until it has doubled in size. (This may take 3 to 10 hours depending on the ambient room temperature.) Place the dough in the refrigerator for an overnight cold proof.

Shape and final proof (20 minutes active, 2–8 hours final proof)

1. The next day, prepare a baking sheet with parchment paper.
2. Use a rolling pin to roll the dough out into a 14 × 18-inch (36 × 46cm) rectangle. Use a bench scraper, pizza cutter, or sharp knife to cut the rectangle into twelve smaller rectangles, each measuring roughly 3 × 7 inches (8 × 18cm).
3. Use the bench scraper to cut thin strips of dough (lengthwise) along the top half of each rectangle. Place one chocolate stick on the bottom (uncut) part of the dough. Fold the dough over the chocolate stick. Once you have folded the dough over the chocolate stick once, place another chocolate stick on the rectangle and continue rolling to form a log. (The buns will look like a wool roll.) Place the buns on the baking sheet.
4. Cover the buns with plastic wrap and let them proof until they're doubled in size and a finger-poke test reveals a slow return of the dough. (This may take 2 to 8 hours depending on the ambient room temperature.) (See Note.)

Bake and store the buns (20–25 minutes)

1. Preheat the oven to 375°F (190°C).
2. Whisk the remaining egg in a small bowl. Brush the tops of the buns with the egg wash.
3. Bake for 20 to 25 minutes or until golden and the internal temperature measures 195°F (91°C). (These are best enjoyed warm out of the oven.)
4. Store the buns in an airtight container for up to 3 days or freeze in a freezer bag for up to 2 months. These are best warmed in the microwave or oven prior to eating.

Note: The addition of cinnamon may slow the fermentation process.

Total time: 42 hours
Active prep time: 1 hour 15 minutes
Baking time: 16–20 minutes
Makes: 16 buns

SPECIAL EQUIPMENT

Stand mixer fitted with a dough hook (optional)

INGREDIENTS

Sweet, stiff starter

50g unfed 100%-hydration sourdough starter
66g tap water
20g granulated sugar
120g all-purpose flour

Dough

160g tap water
160g any type of milk (I use 2%)
All of the sweet stiff starter
115g granulated sugar
3 medium eggs, divided
8g sea salt
600g bread flour
Zest from 3 lemons
4g ground cardamom
100g unsalted butter, softened

Topping

Poppy seeds (optional)

Lemon Cardamom Buns

Soft, fragrant, and perfectly sweet, these buns combine the bright citrus flavor of lemon zest with the warm spice of cardamom. Enjoy these with a pat of butter for breakfast or with some drizzled honey or a spoonful of lemon curd for a sweet finish. A sweet sourdough starter adds depth and complexity, making them a delightful treat for any occasion.

Prepare the sweet stiff starter (5 minutes, 12 hours rise)

1. Prepare the sweet stiff starter the night before making the dough by mixing all starter ingredients together in a 1-liter (34fl oz) container. Cover the starter with plastic wrap and let it rise until at peak or has just started to fall, at least 12 hours.

Make and proof the dough (30 minutes active, 4–8 hours bulk proof at room temperature, overnight cold proof)

1. The next morning, in a medium bowl or the bowl of a stand mixer, combine the water, milk, starter, sugar, 2 eggs, salt, flour, lemon zest, and ground cardamom. Mix on low for 10 minutes. Alternatively, knead by hand for 15 minutes until the ingredients are fully incorporated.
2. Gradually add the butter to the dough, 1 to 2 tablespoons at a time, and knead until the butter is fully incorporated after each addition. Knead by hand or in the stand mixer for 10 minutes until the dough is smooth and elastic. Cover the dough with a bowl cover or plastic wrap and let it rest for 1 hour.
3. *(Optional step for gluten development for a more shreddable crumb. If you wish to skip this step, proceed to step 4.)* Once 1 hour has elapsed, perform a coil fold (p. 35). Perform two more coil folds in 30-minute intervals.
4. Cover the dough with a bowl cover or plastic wrap and allow the dough to proof at room temperature until it has doubled in volume. (This may take 4 to 8 hours depending on the ambient room temperature.) Place the covered dough in the refrigerator for an overnight cold proof.

Shape and final proof (40 minutes active, 4–6 hours final proof)

1. The next morning, line two baking sheets with parchment paper.
2. Use a bench scraper to divide the cold dough into sixteen equal-size portions. Gently shape each portion into a round bun, dusting with additional flour if needed to avoid sticking. Optionally, you can tie these loosely with 3 strands of butcher's twine to create a pumpkin shape.
3. Arrange the shaped buns on the baking sheets, leaving space for expansion. Cover with a tea towel and proof at room temperature until doubled in size, puffy, and a finger-poke test reveals a slow return of the dough. (This may take 4 to 6 hours depending on the ambient room temperature.)

Bake and store the buns (16–20 minutes)

1. Preheat the oven to 375°F (190°C).
2. Whisk the remaining egg in a small bowl. Use a pastry brush to brush the buns with the egg wash, then sprinkle the poppy seeds (if using) over the tops of the buns.
3. Bake for 16 to 20 minutes or until the buns are golden brown and their internal temperature reaches 195°F (91°C). Cool the buns on a wire rack.
4. Store at room temperature in a resealable bag for up to 3 days or in an airtight container or freezer bag for up to 2 months.

CHAPTER 9

Sourdough-Discard Breads

Total time:
3 hours 15 minutes
Active prep time:
20 minutes
Cooking time: 12 minutes
Makes: 12 crumpets

SPECIAL EQUIPMENT

Four 3-inch diameter × 1.5-inch tall (7.5cm diameter × 3.75cm tall) stainless-steel baking rings
Stainless steel tongs

INGREDIENTS

90g 2% milk
235g tap water, divided
5g granulated sugar
2g active dry yeast
200g all-purpose flour
4g fine sea salt
75g 100%-hydration sourdough starter (at peak or discard)
3g baking soda

Morning Crumpets

Crumpets are the perfect vessels for butter, melting into the deep crevices all the way to the bottom, making for a warm and tasty snack. The sourdough discard in this recipe brings added depth of flavor to the crumpets. If you're not eating these fresh from the skillet, be sure to toast them up and eat them with a knob of butter.

Mix batter and rest (5 minutes active, 2 hours rest at room temperature)

1. Warm the milk and 90 grams of water in the microwave in a small bowl. (Make sure it is not warmer than 100°F [38°C].) Add the sugar and yeast to the mixture and stir to combine. Let the mixture sit for 10 minutes to allow the yeast to bloom.
2. To a medium bowl, add the flour and salt. Stir to combine. Once the yeast-milk mixture has bloomed, add it to the flour along with the sourdough discard. Mix with a dough whisk, wooden spoon, or by hand until a wet dough has formed. (No need to knead it, we are not trying to develop the gluten!) Cover with a bowl cover or plastic wrap and let the mixture rest in a warm environment for 2 hours. If your home is cool, place the covered bowl in the oven with the light on.
3. After 2 hours, in a small bowl, dissolve the baking soda in 145 grams of water. Add this mixture to the dough mixture and stir with a whisk until just a few small lumps remain. Cover and let the batter rest in a warm environment for 30 minutes. The rested batter should appear foamy on top. If it hasn't reached this state, let it rest for another 10 minutes.

Cook and store (36 minutes, 12 minutes per batch)

1. Once the batter is foamy (around 30 to 40 minutes), preheat a cast-iron pan or griddle over medium-low heat.
2. Prepare the baking rings by spraying with cooking spray or coating them with butter or oil. Place the prepared rings in the pan to warm them.
3. Once the rings are warm, spoon the bubbly batter into the rings until they are about a third full. Cook for about 10 minutes. (You should notice the conventional crumpet bubbles forming on the surface.) Optionally, if the bubbles are not popping, you can pop the surfaces with a toothpick or skewer.
4. Remove the rings with a pair of heat-safe tongs, flip the crumpet, and cook for 1 to 2 minutes more to brown the tops. These crumpets are best enjoyed while warm!
5. Store the crumpets in an airtight container in the refrigerator for up to 4 days or freeze up to 2 months in an airtight container or freezer bag with wax or parchment paper placed between each crumpet for easy separation. Warm in the toaster.

Total time: 55 minutes
Active prep time: 15 minutes
Bake time: 15–18 minutes
Makes: about 12 oatcakes

SPECIAL EQUIPMENT
Food processor or blender

INGREDIENTS
300g uncooked rolled oats
70g light brown sugar
4g sea salt
3g baking soda
85g room-temperature unsalted butter, cubed
100g 100%-hydration sourdough starter (at peak or discard)

Two-Shores Oatcakes

These oatcakes are a marriage of two traditions—Scottish and Nova Scotian—inspiring the name "two shores." The Scottish version is savory and rustic, made with blitzed rolled oats; whereas the Nova Scotian oatcake is heartier and sweet, made with whole rolled oats. My recipe blends the two traditions and adds my personal touch of sourdough starter, creating a delightful, balanced combination. They have become a staple in my kitchen—simple, yet comforting and enjoyed by all.

Make the dough (10 minutes active, 30 minutes freezer)

1. Blitz the rolled oats in a food processor or blender until they are ground to your preferred texture. (I prefer a finely ground oat in this recipe.)
2. Add the processed oats, brown sugar, salt, and baking soda to a medium bowl. Stir until fully combined.
3. Add the cubed butter and press into the oat mixture with your fingers.
4. Using a fork or dough whisk, stir in the starter until fully combined. (This is not a very wet dough and will resemble cookie dough more than bread dough.)
5. Pour dough onto a 12-inch (30cm) square of plastic wrap. Wrap the plastic around the dough and make a cylinder about 3 to 4 inches (8 to 10cm) in diameter. Place the dough in the freezer for 30 minutes.

Bake and store the oatcakes (15–18 minutes)

1. While dough is in the freezer, preheat the oven to 375°F (190°C). Prepare a baking sheet by lining it with parchment paper.
2. After 30 minutes, unwrap the cold dough and use a sharp knife to cut it into twelve equal-size rounds and place on the baking sheet. If you prefer, you may use a rolling pin to roll the oatcakes thinner.
3. Bake for 15 to 18 minutes or until the undersides are golden brown. Cool on a wire rack for 10 to 15 minutes.
4. Top with toppings of choice (I like to use chocolate ganache and sprinkles) or just enjoy them plain with a cup of tea.

Total time: about 1 hour 30 minutes
Active prep time: 20 minutes
Bake time: 60–75 minutes
Makes: 1 loaf

SPECIAL EQUIPMENT

One standard loaf pan (about 9 × 5-inches [23 × 13cm])

INGREDIENTS

330g overripe bananas (about 3 medium)
185g light brown sugar
105g melted butter or neutral oil (like avocado oil)
4g vanilla extract
2 medium eggs
67g any type of milk (I use 2%)
90g 100%-hydration sourdough starter (at peak or discard)
260g all-purpose flour
5g baking soda
1g sea salt
1.5g ground cinnamon
100g chopped walnuts (optional)

My Favorite Banana Bread

This banana bread has fast become a staple in my home and is perfect for breakfast or a midday snack. The walnuts can easily be substituted with blueberries (fresh or frozen) or semisweet chocolate chips. Whatever your taste may be, you're sure to enjoy this moist, sourdough-enriched banana bread.

Preheat the oven and prep the pan (5 minutes active)

1. Preheat the oven to 350°F (175°C).
2. Cut a strip of parchment paper to fit the length of your loaf pan. Line the pan with it, allowing some overhang. Lightly butter the exposed sides of the pan not covered by the parchment paper.

Make the batter (7–10 minutes active)

1. In a large bowl, mash the bananas with a fork or whisk until smooth.
2. Add the sugar, melted butter (or oil), vanilla extract, and eggs to the bowl. Whisk until fully combined.
3. In a separate medium bowl, combine the milk and the sourdough starter. Whisk until fully combined. Add this mixture to the banana mixture and whisk until fully combined.
4. In a medium bowl, stir together the flour, baking soda, salt, and cinnamon.
5. Add the dry mixture to the wet mixture and fold gently with a silicone spatula until just combined. Do not overmix!
6. Fold in the chopped walnuts (if using).

Bake and store the bread (60–75 minutes)

1. Pour the batter into the prepared loaf pan.
2. Bake for 60 to 75 minutes or until the top is golden brown or internal temperature measures 205°F (96°C). If the top browns too quickly, tent the loaf pan with foil for the last 15 to 20 minutes of baking.
3. Transfer the pan to a wire rack and allow it to cool for 1 to 2 hours before slicing.
4. Store the banana bread at room temperature in an airtight container or bag for up to 3 days or slice and freeze for up to 2 months in a freezer bag.

Fluffy Pancakes

Total time: 30 minutes
Active prep time: 30 minutes
Cook time: 4–6 minutes
Makes: 15 pancakes

SPECIAL EQUIPMENT

Hand mixer (optional)

INGREDIENTS

220g 100%-hydration sourdough starter (at peak or discard)
2 medium eggs
300g any type of milk (I use 2%)
6g vanilla extract
50g unsalted butter, melted
200g all-purpose flour
60g granulated sugar
9g baking powder
6g baking soda
4g fine sea salt

A satisfying way to start the day, these pancakes make excellent use of sourdough discard. Adding a subtle tang and tender texture to each bite, they are the perfect morning treat. They're quick to throw together and extremely versatile. And whether you top them with some yogurt and berries, a pat of butter and pure maple syrup, or a generous dollop of Nutella, they will become a morning favorite.

Make the batter (5–10 minutes active)

1. Warm a large cast-iron pan or griddle over medium heat. Grease the pan with a small pat of butter or cooking spray.
2. Using a hand mixer or whisk, mix together sourdough starter, eggs, milk, vanilla, and butter in a medium bowl. Mix until fully combined.
3. In a separate medium bowl, stir together the dry ingredients until cohesive.
4. Add the dry ingredients to the wet ingredients and stir with a silicone spatula or wooden spoon until just combined. (Do not overmix; a few small lumps in the batter is fine.)

Cook and store the pancakes (15–20 minutes active)

1. Ladle the batter into the pancake size of choice. Flip the pancake after 2 to 3 minutes or when you start to see bubbles forming on the surface of the batter. Cook for 1 to 2 minutes on the other side.
2. Serve with your toppings of choice.
3. Store the pancakes in an airtight container in the refrigerator for up to 3 days or freeze up to 2 months in an airtight container or freezer bag with wax or parchment paper placed between each pancake for easy separation. Warm in the toaster or microwave.

Total time: 45–60 minutes
Active prep time: 10 minutes
Cook time: 25–35 minutes
Makes: 8 waffles

SPECIAL EQUIPMENT

Waffle iron

INGREDIENTS

450g any type of milk (I use 2%)
130g 100%-hydration sourdough starter (at peak or discard)
2 medium eggs
113g unsalted butter, melted
8g vanilla extract
255g all-purpose flour
40g granulated sugar
16g baking powder
4g fine sea salt

Golden Waffles

These sourdough discard waffles are crisp on the outside and fluffy on the inside. They're easy to make and can be served with a variety of toppings. If you're looking for a lazy weekend breakfast, or even a make-ahead option to warm up in the toaster, look no further than this simple recipe!

Preheat waffle iron and mix the batter (5–10 minutes active)

1. Preheat your waffle iron on high.
2. In a medium bowl, combine the milk, starter, eggs, butter, and vanilla extract. Whisk until cohesive and no lumps from the starter remain.
3. In a separate medium bowl, stir together the dry ingredients until cohesive.
4. Add the dry ingredients to the wet and stir with a silicone spatula or wooden spoon until just combined. (Do not overmix; a few small lumps in the batter is fine.)

Cook and store the waffles (25–35 minutes active)

1. If you prefer crispy waffles and your waffle iron is nonstick, do not grease the iron. If you prefer a softer waffle, grease the iron with cooking spray or butter.
2. Pour about ⅓ to ½ cup of the batter into the hot waffle iron. Cook until the waffle is golden brown.
3. Gently remove the waffle from the iron with a fork or stainless-steel tongs and place it on a wire rack until ready to serve. Repeat with the remaining batter.
4. Store the waffles in an airtight container in the refrigerator for up to 3 days or freeze up to 2 months in an airtight container or freezer bag with wax or parchment paper placed between each waffle for easy separation. Warm in the toaster.

Total time: 45–60 minutes
Prep time: 25 minutes
Cook time: 18–22 minutes
Makes: 8 scones

SPECIAL EQUIPMENT
Box grater

INGREDIENTS

Homemade buttermilk (see Note)
95g any type of milk (I use 2%)
5g white vinegar

Dough
340g all-purpose flour
90g granulated sugar
20g baking powder
3g fine sea salt
150g frozen unsalted butter
1 medium egg
All of the homemade buttermilk (100g)
125g 100%-hydration sourdough starter (at peak or discard)
3g vanilla extract

Toppings (optional)
Egg (for egg wash)
Turbinado sugar

Classic Buttermilk Scones

These scones are, hands down, one of my favorite ways to use sourdough discard. They're tender, buttery, and cloud soft, and each bite feels like a little indulgence. I am a big fan of buttermilk scones, but since most people do not keep buttermilk on hand, I have included an easy homemade version using just milk and vinegar. The dough comes together effortlessly, making these perfect for a laid-back breakfast or afternoon treat. Serve warm with butter and a spoonful of jam or go all out with clotted cream and fresh preserves!

Preheat the oven, make the homemade buttermilk, and mix the dough (15–20 minute active)

1. Preheat your oven 400°F (205°C). Prepare a baking sheet by lining it with parchment paper.
2. In a medium bowl, mix together the milk and vinegar. Let it sit for 5 to 10 minutes to allow it to curdle. Set aside.
3. In a large bowl, whisk together flour, sugar, baking powder, and salt.
4. Use a box grater to grate the frozen butter. Add the frozen, grated butter to the flour mixture and combine with your fingers.
5. In a medium bowl, whisk together the egg, homemade buttermilk, starter, and vanilla extract until cohesive and no lumps from the starter remain.
6. Add the wet ingredients to the dry ingredients and stir together with a fork until just combined and everything appears moistened.

Shape the scones (5 minutes active)

1. Turn the dough out onto a lightly floured work surface and gently work it into a ball. Press the ball into a 1-inch (2.5cm) thick disc.
2. Using a sharp knife or bench scraper, cut the disc into eight evenly sized wedges.
3. Evenly distribute the wedges on the baking sheet.
4. If desired, whisk the egg in a small bowl and brush the wedges with the egg wash. Sprinkle the wedges with the turbinado sugar.

Bake and store (18–22 minutes)

1. Bake for 18 to 22 minutes or until the edges of the tops of the scones are golden brown.
2. Cool on a wire rack for a few minutes before serving.
3. Store the scones in an airtight container at room temperature for up to 3 days or freeze for up to 2 months in an airtight container or freezer bag.

Note:
If you have buttermilk on hand, you are welcome to use that. However, most homes likely do not have buttermilk, so I have included the simple recipe to make your own!

Raisin Bran Muffins

Total time: 30 minutes
Active prep time: 5–10 minutes
Baking time: 20 minutes
Makes: about 12 muffins

SPECIAL EQUIPMENT

Standard-size 12-cup muffin tin

INGREDIENTS

90g neutral oil (I use avocado oil)
205g any type of milk (I use 2%)
10g white vinegar
120g 100% hydration sourdough starter (at peak or discard)
3g vanilla extract
2 medium eggs
65g fancy molasses
4g sea salt
135g light brown sugar
120g wheat bran
100g all-purpose flour
130g whole wheat flour
6g baking powder
5g baking soda
150g any type of raisins

These hearty muffins are a nourishing way to start your day. Packed with fiber from the wheat bran and a subtle tang from the sourdough starter, they make for a wholesome and delicious snack. Enjoy these warm out of the oven or prepare in advance for an easy start to your morning.

Make the batter (5–10 minutes active)

1. Preheat the oven to 400°F (205°C). Line the muffin tin with muffin liners or spray with cooking spray.
2. Add the oil, milk, vinegar, starter, vanilla extract, eggs, molasses, salt, and sugar to a large mixing bowl. Whisk until fully combined.
3. In a medium bowl, whisk together the wheat bran, all-purpose and whole wheat flours, baking powder, and baking soda.
4. Add the dry ingredients to the wet ingredients and stir with a wooden spoon until fully combined. (Do not overmix!)
5. Fold in the raisins.

Bake and store the muffins (19 minutes)

1. Fill the muffin cups ¾ full with the batter.
2. Bake for 7 minutes at 400°F (205°C), then lower the temperature to 350°F (175°C) and bake for an additional 12 minutes.
3. Let the muffins cool on a wire rack for 15 minutes. These are best enjoyed warm.
4. Store in an airtight container for up to 5 days or freeze in a freezer bag for up to 2 months.

Total time: 50 minutes
Active prep time: 15 minutes
Bake time: 25–35 minutes
Makes: 16 small or 9 medium brownies

SPECIAL EQUIPMENT

One 9 × 9 × 2-inch (23 × 23 × 5cm) baking pan

INGREDIENTS

160g unsalted butter
310g extra-fine granulated sugar
173g semisweet chocolate chips, divided
50g unsweetened cocoa powder
135g 100%-hydration sourdough starter (discard or peaked)
2 medium eggs
1 medium egg yolk
8g vanilla extract
4g fine sea salt
150g all-purpose flour

Fudgy Brownies

These irresistible brownies transform your sourdough discard into fudgy bliss! Each bite is a balance of flavor and texture, from the semisweet chocolate bursts to the mild tang from the sourdough discard. It will satisfy even the deepest of chocolate cravings. If you're looking for a fast and decadent treat, this recipe is the one for you!

Preheat the oven and mix the batter (15 minutes)

1. Preheat the oven to 350°F (175°C). Grease the baking pan with unsalted butter or cooking spray.
2. In a medium, microwave-safe mixing bowl, melt the butter in the microwave on high in 30-second intervals.
3. Once the butter is fully melted, add the sugar and stir with a silicone spatula until fully combined. Place the bowl back in the microwave and heat on high in 30-second intervals until the sugar is fully dissolved, stirring with the spatula in between intervals to help dissolve the sugar.
4. Add 113 grams of the chocolate chips to the mixture and stir. Return the bowl to the microwave and heat in 30-second intervals, stirring in between, until the chocolate is fully melted and mixture is glossy. Whisk in the cocoa powder.
5. To the butter and chocolate mixture, add the starter, eggs, egg yolk, vanilla, and salt. Whisk until completely combined.
6. Using the silicone spatula, fold in the flour until just combined. Add the remaining 60 grams chocolate chips and fold until evenly distributed.

Bake and store the brownies (25–35 minutes)

1. Pour the batter into the prepared pan and smooth the top with the silicone spatula.
2. Bake for 25 to 35 minutes or until a toothpick inserted in the center comes out with soft crumbs, not wet batter.
3. Cool the brownies in the pan on a wire rack for 30 minutes before slicing. (For cleaner slices, allow to cool for 1 to 2 hours.)
4. Store the brownies in an airtight container for up to 3 days or freeze for up to 2 months in an airtight container or freezer bag.

Total time: 2½–24½ hours
Active prep time: 10 minutes
Baking time: 9–12 minutes
Makes: 16 cookies

SPECIAL EQUIPMENT

Stand mixer fitted with a paddle attachment (or electric mixer)
Cookie scoop, size #30 (optional)

INGREDIENTS

113g room-temperature unsalted butter
183g light brown sugar
100g 100%-hydration sourdough starter (at peak or discard)
2 medium eggs
1 tsp vanilla extract
150g all-purpose flour
1 tsp baking powder
1 tsp fine sea salt
65g unsweetened cocoa powder
55g semisweet chocolate chunks or chips

Double Chocolate Brownie Cookies

If you have a hankering for some chocolate, these rich, chewy, deeply chocolatey brownie cookies are the perfect way to use up sourdough discard—each bite is a decadent treat. The flavor combination of the smooth chocolate and tangy sourdough discard is what makes these luxurious cookies the perfect sweet. Try pairing them with a dollop of vanilla whipped cream or ice cream.

Mix and chill the dough (5–10 minutes active, 2–24 hours in refrigerator)

1. Prepare two cookie sheets by lining them with parchment paper.
2. Add the butter and brown sugar to a medium bowl or the bowl of a stand mixer. Whip until light, about 4 to 5 minutes.
3. Add the starter, eggs, and vanilla. Beat until fully combined.
4. In a separate medium bowl, stir together the flour, baking powder, salt, and cocoa powder.
5. Add the flour mixture to the butter mixture and mix on low until just combined. (Make sure there are no dry patches, but do not overmix.)
6. Gently fold in the chocolate chunks or chips.
7. Using a cookie scoop or tablespoon, portion the dough into sixteen cookies and place them on the cookie sheets spaced 2.5 inches (6cm) apart.
8. Cover with plastic wrap and refrigerate for 2 to 24 hours. (Refrigerating the cookie dough improves the texture of the dough so the cookie comes out thicker and chewier. It also results in a more pronounced flavor.)

Bake and store the cookies (9–12 minutes)

1. Preheat the oven to 350°F (175°C).
2. Bake for 9 to 12 minutes or until the edges are set and the center is still soft but no longer shiny. Remove from the oven and allow the cookies to rest on the cookie sheet for 5 to 10 minutes before transferring them to a cooling rack.
3. Store the cookies in an airtight container for up to 1 week, freeze the unbaked cookies for up to 2 months, or freeze the baked cookies in a freezer bag for up to 2 months.

Cloud Crullers

Total time:
2 hours 10 minutes
Active prep time:
50–60 minutes
Cooking time:
20–30 minutes
Makes: 10–12 crullers

SPECIAL EQUIPMENT

Piping bag with a large star tip
Oil thermometer (optional)
Stainless steel tongs
Slotted spoon or stainless-steel spider strainer

INGREDIENTS

Dough

30g tap water
140g whole milk
100g 100%-hydration sourdough starter (at peak or discard)
25g granulated sugar
6g sea salt
155g unsalted butter
190g all-purpose flour
2–3 medium eggs, beaten and divided
950–1,200g vegetable oil, for frying (the oil should be 2 inches [5cm] deep in the pot)

Glaze

120g confectioners' sugar
2g vanilla extract
15–30g any type of milk (I use 2%)
Pinch of fine sea salt

These crispy, golden crullers are a delightful twist on a classic fried pastry, made by creating the sourdough version of *pâte à choux*. They are an indulgent and delicious way to use your sourdough discard. With a delicate and crisp exterior, fluffy interior, and a sweet glaze on top, they're the perfect treat to serve warm for breakfast, brunch, or dessert.

Prepare the dough/choux (30 minutes active, 1 hour in refrigerator)

1. In a medium saucepan, combine the water, milk, starter, sugar, salt, and butter. Heat over medium, stirring constantly, just until the mixture comes to a boil.
2. Remove the saucepan from the heat and add the flour all at once. Stir vigorously with a wooden spoon until a ball forms and a light film coats the bottom of the saucepan.
3. Transfer the dough to a bowl and spread it out to cool slightly, about 10 minutes.
4. Once the dough is cool, add a small amount of beaten eggs and stir with a wooden spoon until fully incorporated. Keep adding eggs until the dough is smooth, glossy, and holds a V shape when a spatula is lifted from the bowl.
5. Transfer the choux to a piping bag fitted with a large star tip.
6. Place the filled piping bag in the refrigerator for 1 hour to allow the dough to firm up and make it easier to pipe.

Make the glaze, pipe and fry the crullers (30 minutes active)

1. After one hour has elapsed, cut twelve 3.5-inch (9cm) parchment paper squares.
2. Prepare the glaze by mixing all glaze ingredients in a small bowl.
3. Remove the dough from the refrigerator and pipe 3- to 4-inch (8 to 10cm) circles of dough onto the squares of parchment paper.
4. Heat an 8- to 9-inch (20 to 23cm) saucepan filled with 2 inches (5cm) of oil to 350°F (177°C). (Use a candy thermometer to maintain the temperature.)
5. Carefully place the parchment paper squares dough-side down into the oil. After a few seconds, gently peel away the parchment using tongs.
6. Fry two crullers at a time, cooking for 2 to 3 minutes on each side. Flip the crullers with a slotted spoon.
7. Using the slotted spoon, remove the crullers from the oil and place them on a paper towel–lined plate to drain briefly.

Glaze and store the crullers (10 minutes)

1. While still warm, dip each cruller into the prepared glaze and set them on a wire rack to cool slightly. The crullers are best enjoyed warm, fresh out of the fryer.
2. Glazed crullers should be enjoyed on the same day for optimal texture. Store unglazed crullers in an airtight container at room temperature for up to 1 day or freeze in a freezer bag for up to 1 month.

Total time: 2½ –24½ hours
Active prep time: 10 minutes
Baking time: 9–12 minutes
Makes: 18 cookies

SPECIAL EQUIPMENT

Stand mixer fitted with a paddle attachment (or electric mixer)
Cookie scoop, size #30 (optional)

INGREDIENTS

113g room-temperature unsalted butter
95g granulated sugar
100g light brown sugar
130g 100%-hydration sourdough starter (at peak or discard)
1 medium egg
6g vanilla extract
115g all-purpose flour
100g bread flour
3g baking soda
2g baking powder
3g fine sea salt
225g semisweet chocolate chips

Chewy Chocolate Chip Cookies

There is nothing quite like a classic chocolate chip cookie—especially one with a sourdough twist! These cookies are irresistibly chewy with pools of melty chocolate in every bite. You'll keep going back for more!

Mix and chill the dough (5–10 minutes active, 2–24 hours in the refrigerator)

1. Prepare a cookie sheet by lining it with parchment paper.
2. Add the butter, granulated sugar, and brown sugar to a medium bowl or the bowl of a stand mixer. Whip until light, about 4 to 5 minutes.
3. Add the starter, egg, and vanilla. Beat until fully combined.
4. In a separate medium bowl, stir together all-purpose flour, bread flour, baking soda, baking powder, and salt.
5. Add the flour mixture to the butter mixture and mix on low until combined. (Do not overmix; mix just enough to ensure the dough is completely combined.)
6. Add the chocolate chips and mix on low speed until evenly distributed.
7. Using a cookie scoop or a tablespoon, portion the dough into eighteen cookies and place them on the cookie sheet spaced 2.5 inches (6cm) apart.
8. Cover with plastic wrap and refrigerate for 2 to 24 hours. (The longer rest in the refrigerator produces a more enhanced flavor and chewy texture.)

Bake and store the cookies (9–12 minutes)

1. Preheat the oven to 375°F (190°C).
2. Bake for 9 to 12 minutes or until the cookies are lightly brown at the edges. Remove from the oven and allow the cookies to rest on the cookie sheet for 5 to 10 minutes before transferring to a cooling rack.
3. Store the cookies in an airtight container for up to 1 week, freeze the unbaked cookies for up to 2 months, or freeze the baked cookies in a freezer bag for up to 2 months.

Chewy Peanut Butter Cookies

Total time: 45 minutes
Active prep time: 10 minutes
Baking time: 10–12 minutes
Makes: 18 cookies

SPECIAL EQUIPMENT

Stand mixer fitted with a paddle attachment (or electric mixer)
Cookie scoop, size #30 (optional)

INGREDIENTS

113g room-temperature unsalted butter
35g granulated sugar
150g light brown sugar
300g smooth peanut butter
130g 100%-hydration sourdough starter (at peak or discard)
1 medium egg
6g vanilla extract
110g all-purpose flour
3g baking soda
2g fine sea salt

These sourdough-discard peanut-butter cookies are soft, chewy, and packed with peanut-buttery goodness! The addition of sourdough starter brings a subtle depth of flavor and softness that makes them irresistible. If you're looking for an easy, *fast* way to use up your discard, look no further than this delectable recipe.

Preheat the oven and mix the dough (5–10 minutes active)

1. Preheat the oven to 375°F (190°C). Prepare a cookie sheet by lining it with parchment paper.
2. Add the butter, granulated sugar, brown sugar, and peanut butter to a medium bowl or to the bowl of a stand mixer. Whip until light, about 4 to 5 minutes.
3. Add the starter, egg, and vanilla. Beat until fully combined.
4. In a separate medium bowl, stir together the flour, baking soda, and salt.
5. Add the flour mixture to the butter mixture and mix on low until combined.
6. Using a cookie scoop or a tablespoon, portion the dough into eighteen cookies and place them onto the cookie sheet spaced 2.5 inches (6cm) apart.
7. Use the tines of a fork to gently press down onto each cookie to create hashmarks and help spread the cookie.

Bake and store the cookies (10–12 minutes)

1. Bake for 10 to 12 minutes, or until cookies are lightly browned at the edges. Remove from the oven and allow the cookies to rest on the cookie sheet for 5 minutes before transferring to a cooling rack.
2. Store the cookies in an airtight container for up to 1 week, freeze the unbaked cookies for up to 2 months, or freeze the baked cookies for up to 2 months in an airtight container.

Total time: 30–45 minutes
Active prep time: 20–30 minutes
Baking time: 9–12 minutes
Makes: 40 individual Linzers or 20 jam-filled sandwiches

SPECIAL EQUIPMENT

Stand mixer fitted with a paddle attachment (or electric mixer)
3-inch (8cm) round or fluted cookie cutter
Small heart-, star-, or flower-shaped cookie cutter

INGREDIENTS

Dough

226g room-temperature unsalted butter
100g granulated sugar
36g light brown sugar
100g 100%-hydration sourdough starter (at peak or discard)
6g vanilla extract
250g all-purpose flour
72g almond flour
20g cornstarch
4g fine sea salt

Filling and topping

160g jam of choice (I use raspberry jam)
Confectioners' sugar

Linzer Cookies

These cookies hold a special place in my heart, reminding me of visits to local Eastern European bakeries with my nanny. She would treat me and my sister to Polish plum-filled pączki and delicate Austrian Linzer cookies that were flaky, jam-kissed, and unforgettable. Incorporating sourdough discard into this classic felt like a natural next step, adding complexity and depth to an already nostalgic treat. The buttery crumble and richness of almond in these Linzer cookies is balanced by the tart raspberry jam. You can't help but savor every bite!

Mix and chill the dough (5–10 minutes active, 30–60 minutes in refrigerator)

1. Add the butter, granulated sugar, and brown sugar in a medium bowl or the bowl of a stand mixer. Whip until light, about 4 to 5 minutes.
2. Add the starter and vanilla. Beat until fully combined.
3. To a separate medium bowl, add the all-purpose flour, almond flour, cornstarch, and salt. Mix with a fork until fully combined.
4. Add the flour mixture to the butter mixture and mix on low until combined. (Do not overmix; mix just enough to ensure the dough is completely combined.)
5. Form the dough into two discs, wrap them in plastic wrap, and refrigerate for 30 to 60 minutes.

Roll out, bake, and store the cookies (25–35 minutes)

1. Preheat the oven to 350°F (175°C). Prepare two cookie sheets by lining them with parchment paper.
2. Lightly dust your work surface with flour. Working one disc at a time, roll the disc out into a ⅛-inch-thick (3mm) sheet. Use the cookie cutter to cut the sheet into 3-inch (8cm) circles and then transfer the circles, spaced 2 inches (5cm) apart, to a cookie sheet.
3. Using a small heart-, star-, or flower-shaped cookie cutter or the large end of a piping tip, cut out the middles of half of the cookies and place the middles on a separate parchment-lined cookie sheet.
4. Bake for 9 to 12 minutes or until the cookies are lightly brown at the edges. The cutouts should be baked for about 4 to 5 minutes and eaten while you're assembling the full cookies!
5. Cool on a wire rack for 30 minutes. Once cooled, dust the tops of cookies with the cutouts with confectioner's sugar, then place a small spoonful of jam on the cookie bottoms (the ones without cutouts). Sandwich the sugar-dusted cutout cookies on top of the jam-covered cookies.
6. Store the cookies in an airtight container for up to 1 week.

Total time: 2 hours
Active prep time:
1 hour 35 minutes
Baking time: 18–22 minutes
Makes: 12 turnovers

SPECIAL EQUIPMENT

Pastry cutter (optional)
¾-inch (2cm) small circle or heart-shaped cookie cutter (optional)

INGREDIENTS

Dough

250g all-purpose flour
25g granulated sugar
4g sea salt
250g cold, unsalted butter, cut into 1-inch (2.5cm) cubes
75g tap water
75g 100%-hydration sourdough starter (at peak or discard)
2g apple cider vinegar
1 medium egg, beaten (for egg wash)

Filling

450g fresh strawberries, stems removed and halved
70g granulated sugar
Juice of half a lemon
15g cornstarch

Strawberry glaze

60g confectioners' sugar
30g any type of milk (I use 2%)
70g reserved filling juice
Pinch of salt

Flaky Strawberry Turnovers

These sourdough discard turnovers feature flaky, buttery pastry wrapped around a sweet strawberry filling and finished with a gorgeous pink glaze. Whether you're serving them fresh out of the oven for a brunch, or packing them up for a portable afternoon snack, these turnovers always deliver layers of flaky goodness and delicious jammy filling.

Make the dough (30 minutes active, 2 hours refrigerator)

1. In a medium bowl, whisk together the flour, sugar, and salt. Add the butter cubes and toss to coat. Use a pastry cutter or two butter knives to cut the butter into the flour until pea-size pieces remain. Use your fingers to flatten any large chunks of butter.
2. In a small bowl, stir together the water, starter, and apple cider vinegar. One spoonful at a time, add this liquid to the flour mixture, while mixing by hand just until a shaggy dough forms. (Avoid overmixing!)
3. On a floured surface, roll the dough out into a 10 × 20-inch (25 × 51cm) rectangle. Fold it into thirds, like a letter. Roll out again to the same size and then fold into thirds once more. Wrap the dough in plastic wrap and refrigerate it for 30 minutes.
4. Repeat the folding process two more times, with a 30-minute rest in the refrigerator after each fold.
5. Wrap the dough in plastic wrap and place it in the refrigerator while making the filling.

Make the filling (15 minutes active, 40 minutes refrigerator)

1. In a medium saucepan, combine the strawberries, sugar, lemon juice, and cornstarch. Cook over medium heat, stirring often, until bubbly and thickened, about 4 to 5 minutes.
2. Scoop out 70 grams of the filling juice and set it aside for the glaze.
3. Place the remaining filling in the refrigerator to cool.

Assemble and bake the turnovers (30 minutes)

1. Preheat the oven to 400°F (205°C). Prepare a baking sheet by lining it with parchment paper.
2. Use a rolling pin to roll the chilled dough out into a 14 × 18-inch (36 × 46cm) rectangle and then use a sharp knife to trim the edges for uniformity. Cut the rectangle into 12 smaller, equal-size rectangles that are each about 3 × 7 inches (8 × 18cm).
3. Using a circle cookie cutter or heart cookie cutter, cut out the dough in the middle of the upper half of each rectangle. (Alternatively, you can use a knife to cut slits on the upper half of each rectangle, leaving a ½-inch [1.25cm] border of uncut dough.) Place two tablespoons of the strawberry filling on the lower half, then fold the top half over to cover the filling. Brush the edges with the egg wash, press them together with your fingers, then crimp them with a fork.
4. Place the turnovers on the baking sheet. Brush them with the remaning egg wash.
5. Bake in the preheated oven for 18 to 22 minutes or until golden brown. Let them cool slightly before glazing.

Make the glaze and store the turnovers (5 minutes)

1. In a small bowl, mix the confectioners' sugar and milk until smooth. Add the reserved filling juice and salt, and stir until fully combined.
2. Drizzle or spread the glaze over the warm turnovers. Serve warm and enjoy!
3. Store any unglazed turnovers in an airtight container in the fridge for up to 2 days or freeze in an airtight container for up to 2 months. Reheat in an oven preheated to 335°F (170°C) for 10 minutes.

Total time: 2 hours
Active prep time: 1 hour 35 minutes
Baking time: 18–22 minutes
Makes: 12 turnovers

SPECIAL EQUIPMENT

Pastry cutter (optional)
¾-inch (2cm) small circle cutter or a heart-shaped cookie cutter (optional)

INGREDIENTS

Dough

250g all-purpose flour
25g granulated sugar
4g sea salt
250g cold, unsalted butter, cut into 1-inch (2.5cm) cubes
75g tap water
75g 100%-hydration sourdough starter (active or discard)
2g apple cider vinegar

Filling

400g peeled, cored, and diced apples (about 3 medium apples; I like Honeycrisp or Granny Smith)
70g granulated sugar
Juice of half a lemon
2g ground cinnamon
1g ground ginger
1g ground nutmeg
Pinch of cloves (optional)
10g cornstarch
3g sea salt
2g vanilla extract
1 medium egg (for egg wash)

Royal icing glaze

60g confectioners' sugar
30g any type of milk (I use 2%)
2g vanilla extract
Pinch salt

Flaky Apple Turnovers

If you're more of a traditionalist and prefer your turnovers filled with apples instead of berries, this recipe is the one for you. These sourdough-discard turnovers wrap flaky pastry around a sweet-tart apple filling that's spiced with cinnamon, ginger, and a touch of nutmeg. Whether you enjoy them warm with the vanilla glaze or plain off the tray, these turnovers are comforting, warm, and will be enjoyed by all.

Make the dough (30 minutes active, 2 hours refrigerator)

1. In a medium bowl, whisk together the flour, sugar, and salt. Add the butter cubes and toss to coat. Use a pastry cutter or two butter knives to cut the butter into the flour until only pea-size pieces remain. Use your fingers to flatten any large chunks of butter.
2. In a small bowl, stir together the water, starter, and apple cider vinegar. One spoonful at a time, add the liquid to the flour mixture, while mixing by hand just until a shaggy dough forms. (Avoid overmixing!)
3. On a floured surface, roll the dough out into a 10 × 20-inch (25 × 51cm) rectangle. Fold it into thirds, like a letter. Roll it out again to the same size and then fold it into thirds once more. Wrap the dough in plastic wrap and refrigerate it for 30 minutes.
4. Repeat the folding process two more times with a 30-minute rest in the refrigerator after each fold.
5. Wrap the dough in plastic wrap and place it in the refrigerator while making the filling.

Make the filling (15 minutes active, 40 minutes refrigerator)

1. In a medium saucepan, combine the apples, sugar, lemon juice, cinnamon, ginger, nutmeg, cloves (if using), cornstarch, and salt. Cook over medium heat, stirring occasionally, until the apples have softened slightly and the mixture has thickened, about 8 to 10 minutes. You want the apples tender but not mushy.
2. Remove from the heat and stir in the vanilla.
3. Place the filling in the refrigerator to cool.

Assemble and bake the turnovers (30 minutes)

1. Preheat the oven to 400°F (205°C). Prepare a baking sheet by lining it with parchment paper.
2. Use a rolling pin to roll the chilled dough out into a 5 × 20-inch (13 × 51cm) rectangle and then use a sharp knife to trim the edges for uniformity. Cut the rectangle into twelve smaller, equal-size squares that are each about 5 inches (13cm).
3. Using a small circle cutter or a heart-shaped cookie cutter, cut out the dough in the middle of the upper half of each square. (Alternatively, you can use a knife to cut slits on the upper half of each square, leaving a ½-inch [1.25cm] border of uncut dough.) Place 2 tablespoons of the apple filling on the lower half, then fold the top half over diagonally to cover the filling. Brush the edges with the egg wash, press them together with your fingers, then crimp them with a fork.
4. Place the turnovers on the baking sheet. Brush them with the remaining egg wash.
5. Bake in the preheated oven for 18 to 22 minutes or until golden brown. Let them cool slightly before glazing.

Make the glaze and store the turnovers (5 minutes)

1. In a small bowl, combine the confectioners' sugar, milk, vanilla, and salt. Mix until smooth.
2. Drizzle or spread the glaze over the warm turnovers. Serve warm and enjoy!
3. Store any unglazed turnovers in an airtight container in the fridge for up to 2 days or freeze in an airtight container for up to 2 months. Reheat in an oven preheated to 335°F (170°C) for 10 minutes.

Total time:
1 hour 15 minutes
Active prep time:
15 minutes
Baking time:
55–65 minutes
Makes: 1 loaf

SPECIAL EQUIPMENT

Stand mixer fitted with a whisk attachment (or electric mixer)

One 8.5 × 4.5 × 2-inch (21.5 × 11.5 × 5cm) loaf pan

INGREDIENTS

Batter

113g unsalted butter, softened
150g fine granulated sugar
2 medium eggs
130g 100%-hydration sourdough starter (active or discard)
70g lemon juice (around 2 lemons)
195g all-purpose flour
6g baking powder
1g baking soda
2g fine sea salt
Zest of 2 lemons

Glaze

Juice of 1 lemon
40g fine granulated sugar

Lemon Poke Loaf

One of my go-to recipes for a potluck, this bright and zesty lemon poke loaf comes together quickly and effortlessly. The crumb is tender and moist, with the perfect hit of tartness. While still warm, it's poked and soaked with a tangy lemon glaze, giving every bite a citrus punch.

Prepare the batter (5–10 minutes active)

1. Preheat the oven to 350°F (175°C).
2. Prepare the loaf pan by greasing it with butter, oil, or cooking spray.
3. Add the butter and sugar to a medium bowl or the bowl of a stand mixer. Cream until pale, about 4 to 5 minutes.
4. Add the eggs, one at a time, beating until fully incorporated.
5. Add the sourdough starter and lemon juice and beat until fully incorporated. (Note that the batter may look separated, and that is okay.)
6. In a separate medium bowl, stir together the flour, baking powder, baking soda, salt, and lemon zest.
7. Pour the dry ingredients into the wet ingredients and fold gently until no large lumps remain.

Bake, glaze, and store the loaf (5 minutes active, 55–65 minutes baking)

1. Pour the batter into the prepared loaf pan and bake for 55 to 65 minutes or until a toothpick inserted into the center comes out clean or the internal temperature measures 200°F (93°C).
2. While the loaf is baking, prepare the glaze by combining the lemon juice and sugar in a microwave-safe bowl. Microwave on high for 30-second intervals, removing the bowl after each interval and stirring the glaze. Once all the sugar is dissolved, it is ready to be spooned onto the cake.
3. Remove the loaf from the oven and flip it out onto a wire rack. Poke the top of the loaf with a fork at ½-inch (1.25cm) intervals.
4. Gradually spoon the glaze over the hot loaf until it is all absorbed into the cake.
5. Store leftovers at room temperature in an airtight container for up to 3 days. Store in the refrigerator for up to 1 week or freeze the unglazed loaf in plastic wrap and foil for up to 2 months.

Total time: approximately 3–4 hours
Active prep time: 1 hour 30 minutes
Baking time: 30–40 minutes
Makes: 24 triangles

INGREDIENTS

Dough
60g tap water
95g 100%-hydration sourdough discard
11g extra-virgin olive oil
5g white vinegar
3g sea salt
2g baking powder
175g all-purpose flour

Cornstarch mixture
60g cornstarch
30g all-purpose flour

Spread
85g unsalted butter, melted
55g honey

Filling
300g ricotta cheese
55g honey
1g sea salt
Leaves from 4–5 thyme sprigs

Phyllo Ricotta Triangles

These flaky, golden phyllo pastries are a labor of love with a rewarding payoff. The phyllo is rolled thin and layered with a buttery spread, creating a crispy exterior that is filled with a luscious ricotta filling. This recipe infuses the classic phyllo with a sourdough twist. Whether served warm from the oven or as a snack, these triangles are sure to impress.

Make the dough (30 minutes active, 1–24 hours resting)

1. Combine all the dough ingredients in a large bowl and, using a wooden spoon, mix until cohesive. Knead by hand for 10 minutes or until the dough is smooth and pliable. Cover with a bowl cover or plastic wrap and let rest at room temperature for 1 hour or refrigerate for up to 24 hours.

Divide, shape, and roll the dough (45 minutes active, 1 hour resting)

1. Using a bench scraper or a sharp knife, divide the dough into twelve equal-size portions and then shape each portion into a ball. Cover the dough balls with a tea towel and let them rest for 1 hour at room temperature.
2. Make the cornstarch mixture by mixing the cornstarch and flour in a small bowl.
3. After the resting time is complete, dip one dough ball into the cornstarch mixture and use a rolling pin to roll it out into a rectangle that is approximately 5 × 6 inches (13 × 15cm), adding more cornstarch mixture as needed to prevent sticking.
4. Repeat with the remaining balls, stacking the rolled sheets with a dusting of the cornstarch mixture between each sheet. Cover with a tea towel and let the stacked sheets rest for 1 hour.
5. After 1 hour, roll out the entire stack of dough sheets to a rectangle that measures 9 × 12 inches (23 × 30cm).

Prepare the spread and filling (5 minutes active)

1. Make the spread by combining the melted butter and honey in a small bowl and mixing until smooth. Set aside.
2. Make the filling by combining ricotta, honey, salt, and thyme in a small bowl and mixing until smooth. Set aside.

Assemble and bake the triangles (15 minutes active, 30–40 minutes baking)

1. Preheat the oven to 340°F (170°C). Prepare a baking sheet by lining it with parchment paper.
2. Gently separate one sheet from the stack, being careful not to tear it. Lay the sheet flat and, using a pastry brush, brush it generously with the melted butter spread. Place another sheet on top of the first and brush again with the spread. (There should be only two sheets stacked.)
3. Cut the layered sheets into four equal-size columns. Add a spoonful of the filling at one end of each column and fold the dough over to form a triangle. Continue folding, maintaining the triangular shape. One column will make one triangle. Repeat this process with the remaining columns. Repeat steps 2 and 3 with the remaining sheets.
4. Place the twenty-four assembled triangles on the baking sheet and bake for 30 to 40 minutes or until golden brown and crispy.
5. Store in an airtight container in the refrigerator for up to 3 days. Freeze for up to 2 months in an airtight container or freezer bag. Reheat in an oven preheated to 335°F (170°C) for 10 minutes (20 minutes if from frozen) to restore crispiness.

Total time:
about 40 minutes
Active prep time:
15 minutes
Baking time: 22–27 minutes
Makes: about 50 crackers

INGREDIENTS

300g 100%-hydration sourdough starter (peak or discard)
35g poppyseeds
35g sesame seeds
35g flaxseeds
30g unsalted butter, softened
8g sea salt
90g all-purpose flour, plus extra for dusting
Coarse sea salt, for sprinkling

Seedy Crackers

These crackers are the perfect solution for using up your sourdough discard while creating a delicious, wholesome snack. They're packed with nutritious seeds and are full of flavor and crunch. The process is simple and quick, and the result is a batch of crispy crackers that you can enjoy topped with cheese or peanut butter or simply on their own. Whether you're serving them at a gathering or munching on them for an afternoon snack, they're the perfect balance of savory and satisfying.

Make and roll the dough (15 minutes active)

1. Preheat the oven to 350°F (175°C).
2. Add the starter, poppyseeds, sesame seeds, and flaxseeds to a medium bowl. Mix with a fork until fully combined.
3. Add the softened butter and salt to the mixture, mixing until fully incorporated.
4. Add the flour and mix by hand until the dough comes together. (Be careful not to overmix, as this will result in a tough cracker!)
5. Lightly dust your work surface with flour. Using a rolling pin, roll the dough out onto a 12 x 16-inch (30 x 41cm) piece of parchment paper to an even thickness.
6. Use a pizza cutter or a sharp knife to trim the edges to create a neat rectangle, if desired. Cut the dough into your preferred cracker shapes (I make 1 × 2-inch [2.5 × 5cm] rectangles). Dock (poke) the dough at ⅓-inch (1cm) intervals with a fork to prevent puffing during baking.

Bake and store (22–27 minutes)

1. Transfer the parchment paper with the crackers onto a baking sheet. Sprinkle with coarse sea salt. Bake for 22 to 27 minutes or until golden and crisp.
2. Let the crackers cool completely on a wire rack before storing them in an airtight container. They will stay fresh for up to 2 weeks.

Total time: 35 minutes
Active prep time: 35 minutes
Cooking time: 2–3 minutes
Makes: 4 portions (24 gnocchi/portion)

INGREDIENTS

420g russet potatoes
120g 100%-hydration sourdough starter (active or discard)
2 medium egg yolks
6g sea salt
150g all-purpose flour

Potato Gnocchi

I can't express how much warmth and joy these little potato pillows give me on a brisk winter day. The ease with which they come together is unmatched. If you are looking for a quick, homemade pasta, look no further than this recipe. These tender and comforting little treasures will be enjoyed by all. Pair them with your favorite sauce and you'll have a quick and easy meal!

Boil the potatoes and make the dough (20 minutes)

1. Peel and cut the potatoes into 1.5-inch (4cm) square pieces. Place the pieces in a medium pot filled with cold water and bring the pot to a boil over medium-high heat. Cook the potatoes until a fork inserted in the center of a potato breaks it in two.
2. Drain the potatoes and place them in a large bowl. Using a potato masher or a fork, mash the potatoes until completely smooth and no lumps remain.
3. In a small bowl, mix together the starter and the egg yolks until completely cohesive.
4. Add the starter mixture, salt, and flour to the potatoes.
5. Using your hand or a fork, mix all the ingredients together until cohesive.

Shape and cook the gnocchi (10 minutes shaping, 5 minutes cooking)

1. Fill a medium pot three-quarters full with water and bring to a boil over high heat. Add 1 teaspoon of salt.
2. Using a bench scraper or sharp knife, divide the gnocchi dough into four equal-size pieces. Roll each piece out into a log that is ¾ inch (2cm) in diameter. Use a knife or bench scraper to cut the log into ¾-inch (2cm) pieces.
3. Coat a large skillet or cast-iron skillet with olive oil and set over medium heat.
4. Gently drop the gnocchi into the boiling water and allow to cook until they float, about 2 to 3 minutes.
5. Once the gnocchi are floating, use a slotted spoon to transfer them to the heated pan. Brown the gnocchi on both sides, about 1 to 2 minutes per side. Once they are cooked on both sides, place a spoonful of butter in the pan and toss to coat the gnocchi.
6. Remove the gnocchi from the pan and immediately toss them in your preferred sauce.
7. Store the uncooked gnocchi by freezing them in a zipper-lock freezer bag for up to 2 months to maintain freshness. Cook from frozen by boiling them until they are floating, about 4 minutes.

Total time: 4–12 hours (depending on resting time)
Active prep time: 25 minutes
Cooking time: 2–3 minutes
Makes: 4 portions

SPECIAL EQUIPMENT

Pasta roller or rolling pin
Sharp knife or pasta cutter

INGREDIENTS

3 medium eggs
85g 100%-hydration sourdough starter (at peak or discard)
300g Tipo 00 flour
3g fine sea salt
6g extra-virgin olive oil
Semolina flour, for dusting

Enzo's Pasta

A true family favorite, this pasta recipe is as simple to make as it is satisfying to eat. Tipo 00 flour yields that silky texture due to the fine milling process, but if you do not have Tipo 00 flour you can use all-purpose flour instead. Use this dough to make whatever pasta shape your heart desires!

Make and rest the dough (20–25 minutes active, 30 minutes to 12 hours rest)

1. In a small bowl, using a fork, mix together the eggs and the starter until cohesive.
2. Place the flour directly onto a clean work surface and make a small well in the middle. To the well, add the egg and starter mixture, salt, and olive oil. Mix together in the middle with a fork, slowly incorporating the surrounding flour.
3. Once all the flour has been incorporated, use your hands to knead the dough until smooth and elastic, about 8 to 10 minutes. If the dough feels dry, wet your hands slightly and continue kneading; if it's sticky, dust lightly with flour.
4. Form the dough into a ball and wrap it tightly in plastic wrap. Let it rest at room temperature for 30 minutes or refrigerate overnight (up to 12 hours) to develop flavor and make rolling easier.

Roll and shape (15–20 minutes active)

1. Using a bench scraper or sharp knife, divide the dough into four equal-size pieces.
2. Working with one piece at a time and keeping the rest covered to prevent a skin from forming on the dough, flatten the portion into a rough rectangle and then run it through a pasta roller on the widest setting twice.
3. For even strands, fold the short ends of dough to the middle and then fold over again. Pass the dough twice through each subsequent narrower setting until you reach your desired thickness (usually 1 to 2mm or 1⁄16 inch), dusting lightly with flour prior to each pass. (Alternatively, if you don't have a pasta roller, roll out the dough as thin as possible using a rolling pin.)
4. Using a pasta cutter or a sharp knife, cut the dough into noodles or desired pasta shapes. Once the pasta has been shaped, dust with semolina flour.

Cook and store the pasta (2–3 minutes)

1. Bring a large pot of salted water to a boil. Cook the pasta for 2 to 3 minutes or until al dente.
2. Toss with your favorite sauce and serve immediately.
3. To store, dust the cut uncooked pasta with semolina and refrigerate for up to 1 day, or freeze in nests for up to 1 month in an airtight container or freezer bag.

Cornbread Muffins

Total time: 35 minutes
Active prep time: 15 minutes
Baking time: 18–22 minutes
Makes: 24 muffins

SPECIAL EQUIPMENT

Two 12-cup muffin tins
Cookie scoop

INGREDIENTS

113g unsalted butter, melted
30g neutral oil (I use avocado oil)
170g 100%-hydration sourdough starter (active or discard)
235g any type of milk (I use 2%)
3 medium eggs
240g all-purpose flour
140g finely ground cornmeal
130g fine granulated sugar
18g baking powder
6g fine sea salt

These cornbread muffins are the perfect pairing to a hearty bowl of chili or a warm bowl of soup. I even enjoy them plain, warmed up and slathered with a simple pat of butter. They come together in a jiffy and produce a tender, buttery crumb, making them one of my go-to comfort bakes.

Prepare the batter (5–10 minutes)

1. Preheat the oven to 375°F (190°C).
2. Prepare the muffin tins by lining them with muffin liners or greasing them with cooking spray.
3. In a medium bowl, combine the butter, oil, starter, milk, and eggs. Whisk until completely combined.
4. In a large bowl, combine the flour, cornmeal, sugar, baking powder, and salt. Whisk until well combined.
5. Pour the wet ingredients into the dry ingredients and stir until no lumps remain.

Bake and store the muffins (18–22 minutes)

1. Using a cookie scoop, transfer one scoop into each muffin cup. Bake for 18 to 22 minutes or until a toothpick inserted into the center of a muffin comes out clean or the internal temperature reaches 200°F (93°C).
2. Store the muffins at room temperature in an airtight container for 2 to 3 days or freeze in a freezer bag for up to 2 months.

CHAPTER 10

Decorating Sourdough Bread

Bread Decorating Tools

As with any art form, having the correct set of tools can be the difference between something looking uninspiring and something that looks like a true masterpiece. While sourdough in and of itself can be made with very few tools, having a thoughtful toolkit once you step into the realm of decorating will help you elevate your bread and set it apart. Here are some basic decorating tools that are great to have on hand.

Bread lame (and razor blade)

A high-quality bread lame is essential to bread decorating. If you want to create intricate designs on your breads, you'll want to own a high-quality lame; the better the lame, the more precise your scores will be, and the easier it will be on your hands. I use Wire Monkey UFO lames—their compact size allows me to get closer to the dough for more detailed, controlled scoring. I also prefer to "snip the tip," trimming the lateral notches on the razor blade to prevent the blade from snagging on the dough.

Butcher's twine

Butcher's twine is incredibly versatile for shaping and decorating and creating beautifully sculpted dough. It can be tied around a boule to create a classic pumpkin-shaped loaf, creating deep indentations as the bread expands in the oven. It can also be used to create a floral or wreath design, especially when combined with scoring.

Cookie cutters (star/heart/flower)

Cookie cutters are a wonderful guide for creating symmetry in your designs. Pressing a cutter gently into the dough leaves a faint imprint that can then be traced with your bread lame. By scoring outward from the outline of a cutter, you can easily achieve symmetrical floral or mandala-style patterns.

Flour-dusting wand

A flour-dusting wand is particularly handy for evenly distributing edible powders, like rice powder, cocoa powder, or turmeric powder, onto the surface of your dough without clumps forming. The wand opens to hold a small amount of powder and, when gently shaken, it releases a fine sprinkling of powder across the dough. This not only prevents heavy patches but gives you control over the coverage.

Food tweezers

Food tweezers are a precision tool that I use when creating a seed design or when applying or removing stencils from the dough. They allow me to move or lift elements from the dough or counter without disturbing the surrounding decoration. Tweezers offer a level of control that fingers alone can't provide.

Lazy Susan (rotating turntable)

While by no means necessary, a lazy Susan can make the process of scoring much easier. When you're working the far side of the dough, a lazy Susan can simply be turned to rotate the plate and bring the side of the dough you're working on closer to you. My lazy Susan is over 40 years old and was passed down by my late grandmother. It is well-loved, a little worn, and deeply appreciated.

Sewing or embroidery scissors

A pair of fine-tipped scissors makes it especially easy for creating small squares or chevrons on the surface of your dough. To make squares or chevrons, score two parallel lines on the dough, then place one point of the scissors in each line and snip. Holding the scissors perpendicular to the dough will produce clean squares, while angling them will create a chevron effect. While standard kitchen scissors can work for this, they don't offer the same level of control or fine detail that sewing scissors can offer.

Sewing thread

Sewing thread is an excellent tool for creating straight reference lines on your dough. By pulling the thread taut and pressing it lightly into the dough, you can imprint a guide that can be later traced with your bread lame. This is especially useful for creating geometric or grid-based scoring patterns.

Skewer or scribe

A wooden skewer or scribe is an underrated but highly useful tool for decorating. It allows you to draw out a design on your dough before scoring—almost like sketching with a pencil before committing to paint. Lightly tracing your design with a skewer or scribe allows you to determine placement and ensures symmetry before making the cuts with your lame. Beyond sketching, it can also be used to create small holes in your dough, adding texture and detail that complement scored designs.

Scoring

Scoring is the process of making deliberate cuts on the surface of the dough just before baking. Its primary functional purpose is to control how the dough expands in the oven. As the dough heats in the oven, the gases inside the dough expand rapidly, and without a scored spot to release that pressure the dough can burst unpredictably at its weakest points. By scoring the dough, we can intentionally guide the direction of the expansion.

While scoring isn't strictly necessary, most bakers choose to do it—not only to create uniform expansion, but to create stunning decorative patterns. These designs enhance the visual appeal of the loaf. (We "eat first with our eyes," or so the saying goes.) Decorated loaves are perfect for gifting or sharing. And for many bakers, the act of scoring can be meditative and satisfying—a calming and creative ritual that brings meaning and greater joy to the process.

My first foray into sourdough was inspired by seeing decorated loaves online. If you're feeling ready to experiment with scoring your own dough, the following steps will guide you through the process.

Step 1: Prepare your dough for scoring

1. **Make sure your dough is fully proofed.** A well-proofed dough will be easier to score. It will also ensure the dough expands to its fullest potential.
2. **Shape the dough with care.** Using the shaping techniques in this book will give your loaf proper surface tension, which will lead to beautiful expansion and oven spring.
3. **Freeze the dough in the banneton 1 hour prior to scoring.** Freezing your dough for 1 hour will give you time to create an intricate design without having the dough collapse. Freezing also creates more surface tension on the dough, helping the blade glide cleanly without snagging.

1
2
3
4

Step 2: Create your design

1. **Dust the surface of the dough to create contrast (see image 1).** Lightly dust the entire surface of the dough. You'll want to use a flour-dusting wand or miniature sieve to apply the powder evenly. You can use different colored powders to add a pop of color to your loaves. Here are some colored powders you can use to decorate the surface of your loaf:
   - Rice flour
   - Regular cocoa powder
   - Black cocoa powder
   - Blue butterfly pea–flower powder
   - Purple sweet potato flour
   - Ebony carrot powder
   - Turmeric powder
   - Matcha powder
   - Colored rice flour
2. **Use sewing thread to mark the lines (see image 2).** Sewing thread will help you create straight lines. If you are creating circles or stars, use circle or star cookie cutters for accuracy.
3. **Use a skewer, scribe, or toothpick to lightly draw out your design.** Do this before scoring so you can see what it looks like on the dough first.
4. **Use a razor blade and bread lame to score your designs (see image 3).** A bread lame is a device used to safely contain the razor blade while you score the dough. Having a bread lame can prevent nicks and cuts on your fingers while you are scoring. I use Wire Monkey bread lames, but you can use any lame that you prefer.
5. **Perform a 7-minute or expansion score (see image 4).** After you've created your intricate bread score, pop the dough in a preheated, covered Dutch oven and back in the oven for 7 minutes. When 7 minutes have lapsed, pull the dough out of the oven; the dough should have risen a bit and a skin formed. At this point, you will perform an ***expansion score***. The expansion score is a larger, deeper score that is cut into the dough at depths of around ¾ inch (2cm) and will serve as the point from which your dough will expand. By performing the 7-minute score, you will ensure that your detailed design will remain intact, and the dough will expand from the larger cut.
6. **Finish baking the loaf.** Once you have completed the expansion score, pop the dough back into the covered Dutch oven for 20 to 25 minutes. Once the 20 to 25 minutes have lapsed, uncover the Dutch oven to crisp up and darken the crust.

Make your own colored rice flour
Add a tablespoon of rice flour to a mortar and pestle, then add 2 to 3 drops of gel food coloring. Blend together with a pestle until the color is fully incorporated into the rice flour. You can use this powder to decorate the exterior of the sourdough loaf prior to baking.

Create a three-dimensional design (optional)
To create a three-dimensional design, you can insert small pieces of balled up parchment paper to "elevate" the portions that you cut when you pull the dough out of the oven to do the 7-minute score. This will create an exaggerated lift on the surface of the dough.

Creating Seed Designs

The application of seeds to the surface of your dough not only adds a complexity of flavor to your bread, but it can create a more aesthetically appealing loaf. If you are planning to create a design on the surface of your dough using exclusively seeds, I recommend following these instructions to make the process easier. Note that creating an intricate seed design can take time! I have spent as long as an hour making a seed design. It requires patience, a steady hand, and a keen eye.

With these techniques, you will apply the design to the dough after you shape it. If you are using my sourdough sandwich loaf recipe, you apply the design after the cold proof and before the final room-temperature proof. If you are using my standard sourdough loaf recipe, you will apply the design after the bulk proof and just prior to the cold proof. This means that you must time the seed design to ensure it will be prepared when your dough is ready to be shaped.

Ingredients:

Black sesame seeds
White sesame seeds
Colored sesame seeds (These are achieved by mixing gel food coloring and white sesame seeds together in a sealed zipper-lock bag, and using your fingers to press the gel and the sesame seeds together from the outside of the bag.)
Water or medium egg (for egg wash)

Equipment:

Kitchen tweezers
Small spoon
Toothpick or scribe
Small bowl
Whisk
Pastry brush
Bench scraper
Bread lame

Creating Intricate Seed Designs

1. Determine the seed design and the types of seeds and colors to use. If possible, print your design so you can duplicate it on your dough surface.
2. If you've printed a pattern, place it on a flat surface and pour the required color/type of seeds on to the pattern. (If you're not using a printed pattern, you can just work directly on the flat surface.) Using the small spoon, tweezers, and scribe, arrange the seeds according to the pattern you want to create. Fill in the rest with alternating seeds/colors, as desired (see images 1 and 2).
3. Whisk the egg in a small bowl. (Alternatively, fill the bowl with water.) Brush the surface of the dough with the egg wash or water. (Applying an egg wash will ensure the seeds stick a bit better than if you just use water.) Roll the dough carefully over the seeds, ensuring the top is fully coated (see image 3).
4. Place the dough in the proofing container of your choice. If you are proofing in a banneton, the seeds will go topside-down into the banneton (see image 4). If you are proofing in a loaf pan, your seeds will go topside-up.
5. When it is ready to be baked, create an expansion score (see image 5).
6. Proceed with baking per the recipe instructions.

1
2
3
4
5

Decorating with Stencils, Doilies, and Textured Cloths

One of the simplest methods to make your sourdough bread beautiful is to use a stencil, doily, or textured cloth to create designs. By using contrasting powders, you can layer your design with minimal effort and maximal result. You can purchase a stencil, carve one out by hand, use a doily, textured cloth, or create your own design digitally, and then print it with a Cricut or similar machine. While decorating your bread is not required, with minimal effort, stenciling can make a loaf go from average to stunning.

The instructions that follow outline the process of decorating with a stencil using just a few simple tools. After that, you will find how to decorate your bread with a doily or textured cloth. While they may be similar in style, there are slight differences in the processes that have a big impacts on the end results.

Decorating with Stencils

Stenciling is a simple yet striking way to decorate your sourdough bread using just a piece of paper towel and contrasting powder. To get started, choose a design that you like. You can sketch one by hand, trace a printed image, or download a stencil to print and cut out.

I often find myself searching online for inspiration and design ideas. To find stencils online, try searching:

- Mandala design
- Black-and-white floral design
- Geometric pattern
- Animal stencil

I find searching for bold black-and-white images makes cutting the stencil that much easier.

Equipment:
Bread lame
Small scissors
Boar-bristle pastry brush
Nontoxic markers or food-safe pens or markers (optional)
Printer paper or a thick paper towel
Sewing pins (optional)
Spray bottle
Small spoon
Flour dusting wand (optional)

Ingredients:
Edible powder (rice flour, black cocoa powder, turmeric powder, purple sweet potato powder, blue matcha powder, blue spirulina powder, edible luster dust, butterfly pea powder, red dragon fruit powder)

1. Find a design you like. If you decide to create your own, use nontoxic markers or a food-safe pen to draw your design onto a piece of printer paper or a thick paper towel. Using a fine point blade or scissors, carve out the design.
2. Turn your dough out onto parchment paper. Position the stencil on top of the loaf (see image 1). (Ensure the dough has no residual rice powder on it. If it does, dust it with a boar-bristle pastry brush. If you are using a plastic or paper-towel stencil, you can lightly spray your loaf with a bit of water to keep the stencil in place. If you are using a printer paper stencil, don't spray your loaf as it may result in the paper sticking to the dough. If you find your paper is lifting, stick sewing pins through the paper and into the dough to keep it in place.)
3. Using a spoon or flour dusting wand, dust the loaf with your preferred powders and carefully spread using your fingers (see image 2).
4. Slowly lift the stencil off the dough (see image 3). Try to avoid spilling any excess powder through the holes in the stencil.
5. Create an expansion score in the loaf (see image 4). Bake the loaf per the recipe instructions.

1
2
3
4

1

2

3

4

5

Decorating with Doilies and Textured Cloths

Doilies and textured cloths create beautiful, eye-catching patterns on your bread by pressing gentle ridges and valleys into the dough. These impressions can hold flour or colored powder and add a tactile experience to your loaves.

When choosing a doily, look for one that has larger eyelets. If the eyelets are too small, the design becomes lost due to the presence of too much negative space. I have found some online, but if you have a skill for crocheting, try experimenting with your own designs for a custom look.

When choosing a textured cloth, eyelets are not necessary. Instead, focus on cloths made with a large-gauge yarn, which leaves a bold, dimensional imprint in the dough during cold proofing. Knitted designs can give your loaf a distinctive, one-of-a-kind finish.

Equipment:

Doily or textured cloth
Flour-dusting wand
Bread lame

Ingredients:

Edible powder (rice flour, black cocoa powder, turmeric powder, purple sweet potato powder, blue matcha powder, blue spirulina powder, edible luster dust, butterfly pea powder, red dragon fruit powder)

1. Apply a very light dusting of white rice powder to your doily or textured cloth to prevent it from sticking to your dough. Shape the dough (see image 1).
3. Place the doily or cloth on the surface of the dough and place it topside down into the banneton (see image 2). Alternatively, you can, line your banneton with the doily or cloth and place your dough on top. (The dough will form around the cloth creating a unique texture and pattern when turned out of the banneton.)
3. When the dough is ready to be baked, turn it out onto parchment paper. The doily or textured cloth should remain on the top of the dough (see image 3).
4. Dust the top of the doily with your preferred edible powder (see image 4). If you are using a textured cloth, dust the top of your dough after removing the cloth if you like the appearance of a colored or white cast on your baked loaf.
5. Score the loaf and bake according to the recipe instructions (see image 5).

Creating Three-Dimensional Paint Designs

For those who love to express their artistic side, sourdough can become your canvas in the most delicious way possible. This particular technique transforms ordinary loaves into stunning works of edible art, using a method remarkably similar to Mehndi (henna) artistry—where thickened ink flows through fine openings in specially shaped cones.

The process is simple: Create a colored paste by mixing edible powder with water and flour or mixing flour, water, and gel food coloring. Transfer the paste to a piping bag, and pipe your design directly onto frozen bread dough. As the bread bakes, your artwork becomes permanently etched into the crust, creating a striking three-dimensional pattern that makes each loaf a unique masterpiece.

While this decorative technique is purely aesthetic and entirely optional for successful sourdough making, it offers the perfect opportunity to elevate your baking and satisfy your creative impulses. Whether you're looking to impress guests, explore a new artistic medium, or simply add beauty to your daily bread, three-dimensional painting opens up endless possibilities for personal expression.

Equipment:
Cookie cutter (optional)
Toothpick or scribe
Piping bag or zipper-lock bag
Bread lame
Scissors (optional)

Ingredients (powder-based color):
10g edible powder (rice flour, black cocoa powder, turmeric powder, purple sweet potato powder, blue matcha powder, blue spirulina powder, edible luster dust, butterfly pea powder, red dragon fruit powder)
10g all-purpose flour
20–25g tap water (start with 20g and add more as needed)

Ingredients (gel-based color for more vibrancy):
17g all-purpose flour
20g tap water
Gel food coloring (quantity to match desired vibrancy)

1. Find a design that you want to replicate on your dough.
2. Place your dough in the freezer for 1 hour.
3. For powder-based color: Sift the flour and the edible powder together into a small bowl. Slowly add the water, mixing until smooth. (Start with 20 grams of water and increase a few drops at a time until you get a loose, toothpaste-like consistency that is pipeable but not runny.) Let the mixture sit for 5 to 10 minutes to hydrate fully and thicken slightly. For gel-based color: mix together the flour, water, and gel food coloring. Pour the mixture into a disposable piping bag or zipper-lock bag. Cut 1 mm to 1.5 mm (about 1⁄16 inch) from the tip of the piping bag or the corner of the zipper-lock bag.
4. Remove the dough from the freezer and turn it out onto parchment paper. If desired, use a cookie cutter to create a pattern (see image 1).
5. Use a toothpick or scribe to draw the outline of the design onto the surface of the dough (see image 2).
5. Pipe the design carefully onto the dough (see image 3). (The dough will be quite cold, so the piped design will set quickly.)
6. Create an expansion score (see image 4). Bake according to the recipe instructions.

1
2
3
4

1

2

Braiding

Braiding is an elegant technique that transforms a simple loaf into a visually stunning centerpiece. This method involves carefully slicing off the outer layer of shaped dough, cutting it into three equal-size sections, braiding the strips together, and then flipping the braid back onto the surface of the dough. The result is a three-dimensional braided pattern that not only stands out dramatically from the loaf's surface but creates unique depth and texture.

Traditionally, braids are used on enriched doughs, whereby the braids are created from rolled strands of dough, and the dough is then proofed. But this particular process is done on a loaf of artisan bread to create visual appeal and a unique texture.

Equipment
Bread lame
Small scissors

1. Freeze your dough for 1 hour before braiding.
2. Using the bread lame, create four lengthwise cuts in the dough that are spaced 1 inch (2.5cm) apart. Make a perpendicular cut at one end so you can release the strips of dough (see image 1).
3. Using a sharp knife or bread lame, lift one the strips at the horizontal cut line and begin slicing beneath the surface of the strip so that it slowly detaches from the bulk of the dough. Keep slicing until you nearly reach the end of the strip. The top of the strip should still be attached to the bulk of the dough. Repeat with the remaining strips (see image 2).
4. Carefully flip the strips back onto the bulk of the dough and braid them in a three-strand plait (see image 3).
5. If desired, use scissors to add embellishments (see image 4). Bake per the recipe instructions.

BON APPETIT

Acknowledgments

I have fond memories of reading DK educational books as a child, and I still treasure a collection of them today. So when Brook Farling first reached out to me to discuss a sourdough book, "floored" doesn't begin to capture how I felt. Signing the contract was surreal—equal parts disbelief and joy. To be invited into the DK family as a published author is an honor I hold close to my heart. Brook, thank you for your trust, your guidance, and for championing this project from the start.

To my family: Your unwavering support has meant everything. You've tasted every variation, encouraged every experiment, and stood by me through my near-daily bakes! A heartfelt thank you to my two little ones, whose after-school snacks have largely consisted of recipe tests—and whose joy and curiosity have kept me grounded throughout this process. To my husband, sister, and parents: Your love, belief in me, and encouragement have been foundational. This book would not exist without your steadfast support. To my photographer, Marianne Rothbauer: Thank you for bringing these recipes, and my joy of sourdough, to life through your lens. Your ability to capture the beauty and spirit of baking has elevated this book beyond what I could have ever imagined.

And finally, to my online community: Your enthusiasm, engagement, and kindness have been such a strong source of inspiration. Thank you for welcoming me and Enzo into your lives and for supporting me along this wonderful journey. I am deeply grateful.

Index

A
acetic acid bacteria, 15
all-purpose starter, 18
apple butter, 148
Apple Butter and Candied Walnut Wool Roll, 148
Apple-Cinnamon Focaccia, 118–119
autolyse step, 32

B
babka
  Fluffy Chocolate Babka, 142–143
  Fluffy Cinnamon Babka, 146–147
  Fluffy Poppyseed Babka, 144–145
bagels, Montreal-Style Bagels, 104–105
banana bread, My Favorite Banana Bread, 174–175
baker's percentages, 25
banneton, 29
basic loaves
  Enzo Master Loaf, 52–53
  Enzo Whole Wheat Loaf, 54–55
  Rugbrød, 58–59
  Rye-Blend Loaf, 56–57
batards, shaping, 46
bench scraper, 29
beurrage (butter block), 158, 161
biga, 18
boule shaping, 49
bowl covers, 29
bowl scraper, 29
braiding, 228–229
bread lame, 29, 215
brioche, Buttery Brioche, 84–85
Browned Butter and Flaxseed Loaf, 64–65
brownies, Fudgy Brownies, 184–185
bubbles, 39
buns. *See* rolls and buns
Soft Burger Buns, 94–95
butcher's twine, 215
butter block (beurrage), 158, 161
buttermilk, homemade, 181
Buttery Brioche, 84–85
Buttery Croissants, 158–160
Buttery Paratha, 138–139

C
Candied Ginger and Thyme Sourdough Loaf, 68–69
candied walnuts, 148
cardamom glaze, 156
Cardamom Knots, 156–157
cardamom paste, 156
cast-iron bread cloche, 29
Challah Bread, 82–83
Chewy Chocolate Chip Cookies, 190–191
Chewy Peanut Butter Cookies, 192–193
Chocolate Babka, 142–143
Ciabatta, 98–99
Cinnamon Babka, 146–147
Cinnamon-Raisin Swirl Loaf, 74–75
Enriched Cinnamon-Raisin Swirl Loaf, 86–87
cinnamon spread, 146
cinnamon-sugar filling, 152
Classic Buttermilk Scones, 180–181

Cloud Crullers, 188–189
coil fold, 35
cookie cutters, 215
cookies
  Chewy Chocolate Chip Cookies, 190–191
  Chewy Peanut Butter Cookies, 192–193
  Double Chocolate Brownie Cookies, 186–187
  Linzer Cookies, 194–195
Cornbread Muffins, 210–211
crackers, Seedy Crackers, 204–205
croissants, Buttery Croissants, 158–160
crumpets, Morning Crumpets, 170–171
custard, 161

D

decorating bread loaves
  braiding, 228–229
  doilies, 225
  scoring, 216–219
  seed designs, 220–221
  stencils, 222–223
  textured cloths, 225
  three-dimensional paint designs, 226–227
  tools, 214–215
Demi-Baguettes, 90–91
digital scale, 29
digital thermometer, 29
Soft Dinner Rolls, 92–93
discard breads
  Chewy Chocolate Chip Cookies, 190–191
  Chewy Peanut Butter Cookies, 192–193
  Classic Buttermilk Scones, 180–181
  Cloud Crullers, 188–189
  Cornbread Muffins, 210–211
  Double Chocolate Brownie Cookies, 186–187
  Enzo's Pasta, 208–209
  Flaky Apple Turnovers, 198–199
  Flaky Strawberry Turnovers, 196–197
  Fluffy Pancakes, 176–177
  Fudgy Brownies, 184–185
  Golden Waffles, 178–179
  Lemon Poke Loaf, 200–201
  Linzer Cookies, 194–195
  Morning Crumpets, 170–171
  My Favorite Banana Bread, 174–175
  Phyllo Ricotta Triangles, 202–203
  Potato Gnocchi, 206–207
  Raisin Bran Muffins, 182–183
  Seedy Crackers, 204–205
  Soft Tortillas, 134–135
  Two-Shores Oatcakes, 172–173
doilies, 225
Donair sauce, 132
donuts, Plum-Filled Donuts (Polish Pączki), 152–153
Double Chocolate Brownie Cookies, 186–187
dough handling, 39
Dutch oven, 29

E

edible powder, 222, 225, 226
English Muffins, 102–103
enriched loaves
  Buttery Brioche, 84–85
  Cinnamon-Raisin Swirl Loaf, 86–87
  Fluffy Challah Bread, 82–83
  Honey Whole Wheat Sandwich Bread, 80–81
  Soft White Sandwich Bread, 78–79
Enzo Master Loaf, 52–53
Enzo Whole Wheat Loaf, 54–55
Enzo's Pasta, 208–209

F

feeding the starter, 20, 22
fermentation, 44
  starter, 16–18
filled breads
  Nutella-Filled Buns, 150–151
  Polish Pączki, 152–153
finger-poke test, 39
Flaky Apple Turnovers, 198–199
Flaky Strawberry Turnovers, 196–197
flatbreads
  Apple-Cinnamon Focaccia, 118–119
  Buttery Paratha, 138–139
  Fluffy Turkish Pides, 128–129
  Garlic Fingers with Donair Sauce, 132–133
  Moroccan-Style Msemen, 136–137
  Neapolitan-Style Sourdough Pizzas, 130–131
  Pala Romana, 122–123
  Peach and Goat Cheese Focaccia, 120–121
  Pocket Pitas, 126–127
  Same-Day Sourdough Naan, 124–125
  Soft Tortillas, 134–135
  Tomato-Rosemary Focaccia, 116–117
flaxseed, Browned Butter and Flaxseed Loaf, 64–65
float test, 26
flour
  baker's percentages, 25
  hydration and, 42
  proofing and, 39
  starter, 26
flour-dusting wand, 215
Fluffy Challah Bread, 82–83
Fluffy Chocolate Babka, 142–143
Fluffy Cinnamon Babka, 146–147
Fluffy Overnight Cinnamon Buns, 154–155
Fluffy Pancakes, 176–177
Fluffy Poppyseed Babka, 144–145
Fluffy Turkish Pides, 128–129

focaccia
    Apple-Cinnamon Focaccia, 118–119
    Peach and Goat Cheese Focaccia, 120–121
    Tomato-Rosemary Focaccia, 116–117
food tweezers, 215
Fudgy Brownies, 184–185

G
Garlic Fingers with Donair Sauce, 132–133
Garlic Knots, 96–97
garlic spread, 97
German Soft Pretzels, 110–111
glass bread (Pan de Cristal), 100–101
glazes
    for crullers, 189
    for donuts, 152
    for Lemon Poke Loaf, 201
    for Pain aux Raisins, 161
    Royal Icing, 198
    strawberry, 196
gluten
    autolyse step, 32
    coil fold, 35
    developing, 32–37
    lamination, 37
    slap-and-fold, 36
    starter, 22
    stretch-and-fold, 32
    time passage, 32
Golden Waffles, 178–179
gnocchi, Potato Gnocchi, 206–207

H
hole size, 44
Homemade Buttermilk, 181
Honey Whole Wheat Sandwich Bread, 80–81
hooch, 22, 26
hydration, 12
    baker's percentages, 25
    flour and, 42
    kneading and, 32
    proofing and, 38, 42
    starter, 12

I
icing, 152
inclusions
    Browned Butter and Flaxseed Loaf, 64–65
    Candied Ginger and Thyme Sourdough Loaf, 68–69
    Cinnamon-Raisin Swirl Loaf, 74–75
    Jalapeño Cheddar Loaf, 72–73
    Lemon Poppyseed Loaf, 62–63
    Maple Oat Porridge Loaf, 66–67
    Orange Cranberry Loaf, 70–71

J
Jalapeño Cheddar Loaf, 72–73
jiggliness, 39

K
kneading, gluten development, 32

L
lactic acid bacteria, 15
lamination, 37
Lazy Susan, 215
Lemon Cardamom Buns, 166–167
Lemon Poke Loaf, 200–201
Lemon Poppyseed Loaf, 62–63
levain, 12, 18, 27
    Rugbrød, 58–59
Linzer Cookies, 194–195
liquid, baker's percentages, 25
liquid starter, 19
loaf pan, 29
lye solution for pretzels, 110

M
Maple Oat Porridge Loaf, 66–67
molasses water, 113
mold in starter, 26
Montreal-Style Bagels, 104–105
Morning Crumpets, 170–171
Moroccan-Style Msemen, 136–137
muffins
    Cornbread Muffins, 210–211
    Raisin Bran Muffins, 182–183
My Favorite Banana Bread, 174–175

N
naan, Same-Day Sourdough Naan, 124–125
Neapolitan-Style Sourdough Pizzas, 130–131
Nutella-Filled Buns, 150–151
nuts, candied walnuts, 148

O
oatcakes, Two-Shores Oatcakes, 172–173
Orange Cranberry Loaf, 70–71
orange syrup, 144
Overnight Cinnamon Buns, 154–155
overproofing, 42

P
Pączki, 152–153
Pain aux Raisins, 161–163
Pain Viennois (Vienna bread), 108–109
Pala Romana, 122–123
Pan de Cristal, 100–101

Pancakes, 176–177
paratha, Buttery Paratha, 138–139
pasta
  Enzo's Pasta, 208–209
  Potato Gnocchi, 206–207
pasta madre starter, 19
Peach and Goat Cheese Focaccia, 120–121
Phyllo Ricotta Triangles, 202–203
pides, Fluffy Turkish Pides, 128–129
pizza dough, Neapolitan-Style Sourdough Pizzas, 130–131
Plum-Filled Donuts (Polish Pączki), 152–153
Pocket Pitas, 126–127
poolish, 18
Poppyseed Babka, 144–145
poppyseed spread, 144
Potato Gnocchi, 206–207
Pretzels, 110–111
proofing
  bulk proof, 38
  cold proof, 38, 44
  duration, 44
  elevation and, 38
  fermentation, 44
  final proof, 38
  flour and, 39
  gumminess, 44
  hole size, 44
  hydration and, 38, 42
  overproofing, 42
  sourness, 44
  starter and, 39
  temperature and, 38
  well-proofed dough, 39–41
Pumpkin Chocolate Buns, 164–165

R

Raisin Bran Muffins, 182–183
refrigeration, 15
  using starter from, 22
regular starter, 19
rise, 39
rolls and buns
  Ciabatta, 98–99
  Demi-Baguettes, 90–91
  English Muffins, 102–103
  Fluffy Turkish Simits, 112–113
  Garlic Knots, 96–97
  German Soft Pretzels, 110–111
  Montreal-Style Bagels, 104–105
  Pain Viennois (Vienna bread), 108–109
  Pan de Cristal, 100–101
  Salt Butter Rolls (Shio Pan), 106–107
  Soft Burger Buns, 94–95
  Soft Dinner Rolls, 92–93
Royal Icing glaze, 198
Rugbrød, 58–59
Rye-Blend Loaf, 56–57

S

Salt Butter Rolls (Shio Pan), 106–107
Same-Day Sourdough Naan, 124–125
sandwich bread
  Honey Whole Wheat Sandwich Bread, 80–81
  Soft White Sandwich Bread, 78–79
scissors, 215
scones, Classic Buttermilk Scones, 180–181
scoring bread, 216–219
scribe, 215
seed designs, 220–221
seed starter, Rugbrød, 58–59
Seedy Crackers, 204–205
sewing thread, 215
shaping
  batards, 46
  boules, 49
Shio Pan (Salt Butter Rolls), 106–107
simits, Fluffy Turkish Simits, 112–113
simple syrup, 142
skewers, 215
slap-and-fold, 36
Soft Burger Buns, 94–95
Soft Dinner Rolls, 92–93
Soft Tortillas, 134–135
Soft White Sandwich Bread, 78–79
sourness, 44
spreads
  cinnamon spread, 146
  garlic spread, 97
  poppyseed spread, 144
starter
  100% hydration, 12
  acetic acid bacteria, 15
  all-purpose, 18
  amount needed for baking, 21
  as living organism, 15
  bubbles, 22
  discarding, 26, 27
  feeding, 20, 22, 26
  fermentation, 16–18
  float test, 26
  flour, 26
  frequently asked questions, 26–27
  gluten, 22
  hooch, 22, 26
  increasing, 27
  lactic acid bacteria, 15
  levain and, 18
  liquid, 19, 26

making your own, 16–18
microorganisms, 15
mold, 26
odor, 27
pasta madre, 19
peak, 20–21
proofing and, 39
readiness, 18, 26
regular, 19
reviving, 27
science, 15
stiff, 19
storage, 20, 26
temperature, 18
types, 18–19
using from refrigerator, 22
versus levain, 27
water, 26
yeast, 15
stencils, 222–223
stiff starter, 19. *See also* sweet stiff starter
storage
bread, 15
starter, 20, 26
strawberry glaze, 196
stretch-and-fold, 32
sweet sourdough breads
Apple Butter and Candied Walnut Roll, 148
Buttery Croissants, 158–160
Cardamom Knots, 156–157
Fluffy Chocolate Babka, 142–143
Fluffy Cinnamon Babka, 146–147
Fluffy Overnight Cinnamon Buns, 154–155
Fluffy Poppyseed Babka, 144–145
Lemon Cardamom Buns, 166–167
Nutella-Filled Buns, 150–151
Pączki, 152–153
Pain aux Raisins, 161–163
Plum-Filled Donuts (Polish Pączki), 152–153
Pumpkin Chocolate Buns, 164–165
sweet stiff starter
Buttery Brioche, 84
Cardamom Knots, 156
Fluffy Challah Bread, 82
Fluffy Chocolate Babka, 142
Fluffy Cinnamon Babka, 146
Fluffy Overnight Cinnamon Buns, 152
Fluffy Poppyseed Babka, 144
Lemon Cardamom Buns, 166
Pumpkin Chocolate Buns, 165
syrups
orange syrup, 144
simple syrup, 142, 146**T**

T

tangzhong
Fluffy Overnight Cinnamon Buns, 152
Garlic Knots, 97
Soft Burger Buns, 94
Soft Dinner Rolls, 93
textured cloths, 225
three-dimensional paint designs, 226–227
Tomato-Rosemary Focaccia, 116–117
tools and equipment, 29
banneton, 29
bench scraper, 29
bowl covers, 29
bowl scraper, 29
bread lame, 29, 215
butcher's twine, 215
cast-iron bread cloche, 29
cookie cutters, 215
decorating tools, 214–215
digital scale, 29
digital thermometer, 29
Dutch oven, 29
flour-dusting wand, 215
food tweezers, 215
Lazy Susan, 215
loaf pan, 29
scissors, 215
scribe, 215
sewing thread, 215
skewers, 215
tortillas, Soft Tortillas, 134–135
Turkish Pides, 128–129
Turkish Simits, 112–113
turnovers
Flaky Apple Turnovers, 198–199
Flaky Strawberry Turnovers, 196–197
Two-Shores Oatcakes, 172–173

V

Vienna bread (Pain Viennois), 108–109

W–Z

waffles, Golden Waffles, 178–179
walnuts, candied walnuts, 148
water, for starter, 26
White Sandwich Bread, 78–79
whole wheat loaves
Enzo Whole Wheat Loaf, 54–55
Honey Whole Wheat Sandwich Bread, 80–81

yeast, starter, 15
yogurt, 124, 128

About the Author

Rachel Pardoe is a self-taught baker, recipe developer, and the creative force behind Sourdough Enzo. Originally a nurse by profession, Rachel's foray into sourdough baking began in early 2020 and quickly grew into a full-fledged passion and, eventually, a new career. Known for her enticing flavor combinations, whimsical scoring designs, and approachable teaching style, Rachel blends technique with artistry in every bake.

Sourdough Enzo was named after Rachel's beloved starter, Enzo, and was created to celebrate the joy, versatility, and beauty of sourdough baking, from mastering the basics to breaking the rules in the best ways. When she's not elbow-deep in flour, you'll find her dabbling in experimental recipes, doodling in the margins of her notebooks, engaging with her growing community about sourdough, and sharing her baked goods with family and friends.

Rachel is also a proud mom of two kiddos who bring endless inspiration and joy and are often the first to taste test her bakes and provide feedback. This book is an extension of her journey and is meant to inspire, guide, and remind you that sourdough can be nourishing, accessible, and deeply creative.